Bernard Haring

ROAD TO RELEVANCE

"Special attention needs to be given to the development of moral theology. Its scientific exposition should be more thoroughly nourished by scriptural teaching. It should show the nobility of the Christian vocation of the faithful, and their obligation to bring forth fruit in charity for the life of the world."

— Decree on Priestly Formation, #16

DIVISION OF THE SOCIETY OF ST. PAUL

alba house
STATEN ISLAND, N.Y. 10314

Bernard Haring

Road To Relevance

(Translated by Hilda Graef)

240.7
H

Original Title:
Moralverkündigung nach dem Konzil, published by Verlag Gerhard Kaffke.

Translated by:
Hilda Graef

Nihil Obstat:
Daniel V. Flynn, J.C.D.
Censor Librorum

Imprimatur:
Joseph P. O'Brien, S.T.D.
Vicar General, Archdiocese of New York
November 14, 1969

The nihil obstat and imprimatur are official declarations that a book or pamphlet is free of doctrinal or moral error. No implication is contained therein that those who have granted the nihil obstat and imprimatur agree with the contents, opinions or statements expressed.

Library of Congress Catalog Card Number. 79-110592
SBN: 8189-0172-1

Designed, printed and bound in the U.S.A. by the Pauline Fathers and Brothers, 2187 Victory Blvd., Staten Island, N.Y. 10314 as part of their communications apostolate.

PREFACE

After the Second Vatican Council Catholic moral theology and teaching will differ from post-Tridentine theology, which, of course, does not mean that all previous teaching should be jettisoned. But while, from the seventeenth to the nineteenth century, moral theologians considered chiefly the office of the confessor, and particularly under its aspect of judging and exercising control, the view of Vatican II is characterized by dialogue and by preaching the good news of life in Christ Jesus. A careful study of all Council documents will show the same structure of thought in all of them: Christ is at the center, love has the first place, the good news needs a vital answer; there is the "law of faith," a unity of gift and demand, the "law of grace." *The Pastoral Constitution on the Church in the Modern World* will exercise a decisive influence on the moral teaching of the future, especially through its anthropology, which is at the same time personalistic, related to the community and open to history, taking its task in the world seriously precisely because of its eschatological outlook.

The Decree on Priestly Formation (No. 16) offers a brief, but very important program for the renewal of moral theology which, without being conceited, we may well regard as confirming our efforts during the last fifteen years and as a demand to continue on the same lines. First, like all other departments of theology, though with "special attention," moral theology "should also be renewed by livelier contact with the mystery of Christ and the history of salvation."

Further, it "should be more thoroughly nourished by scriptural teaching." Its subject matter is not a mere catalogue of sins, even less is it a list of finicking definitions of what is grave and what is merely venial sin; its real theme is to "show the nobility of the Christian vocation of the faithful, and their obligation to bring forth fruit in charity for the life of the world." Hence the idea of vocation is one of the leading concepts of this Council document. Christian life is supported and inspired by the Lord who calls and gives the vocation. This vocation is sublime; especially in chapter five of the *Dogmatic Constitution on the Church* the Council regards it as a general call to holiness; even though differing according to the measure of grace, it is nevertheless the one vocation to the spiritual law of life in Jesus Christ. The obligation this entails is itself good news, an obligation contained in the "nobility of the Christian vocation." To fulfill this obligation it is not enough to keep the commandments outwardly; Christians must "bring forth fruit in charity" urged by the sacred love of the Lord who calls us.

The term "bring forth fruit" reminds us of the two great systematic accounts of the moral message of the New Testament contained in the farewell speech of Jesus in the Gospel of St. John and in St. Paul's Letter to the Galatians. In close connection with his new commandment Jesus says to his disciples: "I chose you and appointed you that you should go and bear fruit and that your fruit should abide; so that whatever you ask the Father in my name, he may give it to you. This I command you, to love one another" (Jn 15:16-17). In Galatians the word "fruit" is used in connection with the Pauline gospel of the freedom of the Christian through his total obedience to the law of the spirit: "But the fruit of the Spirit is love, joy, patience, kindness, goodness, faithfulness, gentleness, self-control; against such there is no law" (Gal 5:22f).

The expression "to bring forth fruit in charity for the life of the world" emphasizes the social character of Christian morality. We may well here remember the biblical term "for the life of the world" of John 6:51: the Eucharist has been given us for "the life of the world." Hence a morality that is to serve the salvation of the world must always involve the sacramental and Eucharistic structure of the Christian life.

The following chapters were written not only to help pastors and parents to transmit the moral message in the spirit of the Council, but also and especially to give a synthesis in which both word and life proclaim the blessed mystery of Easter.

CONTENTS

1

THE CONTEMPORARY RENEWAL OF
MORAL THEOLOGY

Can there be an essential renewal of theology in the Church, the faithful guardian of revealed truth? Is not Catholic theology by definition the faithful transmission of the one unchangeable truth of faith and its demands on men? If we speak of a renewal of moral theology today, this question must be asked in order to avoid misunderstandings from the very beginning as well as to help us determine the true scope of our work.

In the heavenly Jerusalem we shall no longer need theology, for there we shall see face to face what we see here only, as it were, in a glass darkly. Whether we shall one day be considered worthy of the vision of God will be decided — as far as this depends on ourselves — not least by our honest will to be actively true to our inheritance and our faithful obedience to Christ and the Church, his bride. It also depends on our will to be faithful whether or not the outline of the mirror image, that is our fragmentary knowledge, however vague, remains true.

Courage to be faithful involves humility. Theologians in general and each one individually must realize more and more that they possess their knowledge not in a heavenly manner, but according to their finite state. We do not apprehend truth in one, simple, penetrating glance. We can only try to paraphrase it and to approach it in various ways. The theologian may compare his position to a tower with many windows. From each one he sees only a small section of the marvellous panorama. He must try to look also out of the other windows in order to see several sections. And in the case of those windows that are not accessible to him, he must keep in contact with those who look upon God's world from there. Speaking without metaphors, faithfulness demands that we should remain conscious of the fact that all knowledge is fragmentary and that we must never cling obstinately to a private opinion or the view of one particular school of thought. Theologians and theological schools must remain in contact with each other; it is not enough to live together in the one tower, the one Church.

But the courage to be faithful is not mere earthly courage. It is founded on the Lord's promise to his Church that the gates of hell shall not prevail against it, because it is the fortress of truth. Ultimately theology can be faithful only because the risen Christ has sent the Holy Spirit to his Church and to all the faithful. Thus courage to be faithful also means courage to be obedient to the Church however much the "old man" with his reasoning would like to rebel. Being faithful means constantly struggling against the "flesh," the egocentric way of life and thought, the "wisdom of this world." Being faithful in theology means the same as being faithful in one's Christian life in general, namely to be "led by the Spirit" (cf. Rom 8:14; Gal 5:18). However, as long as we are still pilgrims on the way to the heavenly Jerusalem, we have the courage to admit that we are only on the way to perfect obedience to the Holy Spirit. Theology and theologians are never perfect, they are only on the way. The more they are conscious of this, the more they will always try to be perfectly faithful.

No theologian ought to flatter himself that he has definitely escaped the temptation to curry favor with men. It is his vocation to serve the salvation of men. He must not indulge in vain speculations, but must present the message of salvation to his contemporaries, whether it pleases them or not. But he can serve only if he is faithful. And being faithful means both carefully preserving the inheritance and being aware of the needs of the time, for these, too, come from God and demand faithful service.

Apart from the encyclical *Divino Afflante Spiritu* (Sept. 30, 1943), the *Dogmatic Constitution on Divine Revelation* of Vatican II (Nov. 1965) is the most important document to teach us that all theology must be biblical theology in the fullest sense. Sacred Scripture "is the source of all saving truth and moral teaching" (No. 7). "The Church . . . has always regarded the Scriptures together with sacred tradition as the supreme rule of faith and will ever do so . . . all the preaching of the Church must be nourished and ruled by sacred Scripture" (No. 21). "Sacred theology rests on the written word of God, together with sacred tradition, as its primary and perpetual foundation. By scrutinizing in the light of faith all trust stored up in the mystery of Christ, theology is most powerfully strengthened and constantly rejuvenated by that word. For the sacred Scriptures contain the word of God and, since they are inspired, really are the word of God; and so the study of the sacred page is, as it were, the soul of sacred theology" (No. 24).

Hence it does not suffice to use holy Scripture for proving theological statements, even if we were perfectly ready not to say anything incompatible with the sound exegesis of it. For we must be content to make Scripture a standard to be applied to our theological thought, so to speak as an afterthought. It should rather be the basis for our whole theology, which must teach us the whole of Christian ethics. Catholic moral theology should make it clear at once that its content and its form, its thought structures and its statements owe more to holy Scripture than to any book of law or any philosophical system, whether it be contemporary or Aristotelian.

We would, for example, do a great wrong to St. Augustine or St. Thomas Aquinas if we thought to be faithful to them by merely taking over their Platonic or Aristotelian methods. For their most profound characteristic is their biblical way of thought, their intimate knowledge of Scripture which is evident even when they do not actually quote it. Hence a Catholic theologian must ask himself in conscience whether he is faithful to holy Scripture rather than whether he follows Thomas or Augustine.

Scripture itself gives us clear indications that the moral message may be presented under different leading ideas, though these may be related in content. The Sermon on the Mount shows a different structure from Christ's farewell speech in St. John. But it is quite clear that these two do not contradict, but supplement each other. The authors of the synoptic gospels base Christian morality with its eschatological intent more obviously on their fundamental concept of the kingdom of God, while St. John and St. Paul have a different concept for the same truth.

From the point of view of holy Scripture, however, certain attempts at systematization must simply be regarded as wrong or precarious. Any presentation of Christian morality, for example, which mentions the connection between the saving mystery and moral action not at all or only in passing is alien to holy Scripture. This is true also of a moral teaching that is chiefly concerned with defining minimum obligations while treating God's special gifts of grace more or less as optional additions; for according to Scripture it is the grace of God that teaches us (cf. Tit 2:11f). A moral teaching concerned only with individual salvation and individual duties is also far removed from the spirit of holy Scripture, which is characterized by a wonderful synthesis of individual salvation and the perfection of society. For our concern must always be "for the equipment of the saints, for the work of ministry for building up the body of Christ, until we all attain to the unity of faith and of the knowledge of the Son of God, to mature manhood, to the measure of the stature of the fullness of Christ" (Eph 4:12f). Owing to the wonderful flowering of biblical studies, especially since the encyclical *Divino Afflante Spiritu,* there are today good conditions for a biblical deepening of moral theology. Of special importance is that biblical theology which is not based on later theological systems but presents all the leading ideas of the individual books of the Old and New Testaments.

We should like to ask exegetes to help us even more than before to clarify the originality of the moral message of the Old and New Testaments against the background of the ethical theories and currents of the neighbors of Israel (Cf. *On Divine Revelation,* No. 23). In this connection the Dead Sea scrolls are of great value.

The fact that competent exegetes devote themselves with great energy to moral theology is of paramount importance. Fritz Tillmann, who became a moral theologian while remaining true to his original exegetical interest, became a pioneer in this respect.[1] However, he did not so much produce a systematic synthesis of moral theology for our times as a pres-

---

1. Fritz Tillmann, **Handbuch der katholischen Sittenlehre,** collaborators T. Steinbüchel and T. Müncker, 4 vols., Düsseldorf, 1950; **The Master Calls,** A Handbook of Christian Living (Baltimore: Helicon, 1961).

entation of the leading ideas of the individual inspired authors. We hope that the example of one of our best exegetes, Rudolf Schnackenburg, who realizes that it is not enough for exegetes to inveigh from time to time against non-scriptural systems of moral theology and who therefore offers help in his exegetical studies,[2] will be imitated.

It is a hopeful sign that the Academia Alfonsiana which trains a large number of moral theologians of different nationalities has established two chairs for professional exegetes to lecture on the morality of the Old and New Testaments.[3] Thus no one who has graduated from this Institute will ever get the idea that it is enough to occasionally quote holy Scriptures also.

One of the most urgent tasks of contemporary moral theology is the thorough examination of tradition, for precisely because we must risk an encounter with a modern world of

2. Rudolf Schnackenburg, **Moral Teaching of the New Testament** (New York: Herder and Herder 1965); **God's Rule and Kingdom** (New York: Herder and Herder, 1963); **Die Johannesbriefe**, Freiburg, 1965; id. **Das Johannesevangelium**, part 1, Freiburg, 1965; also C. Spicq, **Théologie morale du Nouveau Testament,** I & II, Paris, 1965; N. Lazure, **Les valeurs morales de la théologie Johannique** (Évangile et Épitres), Rome, 1965.

3. Of the publications of the two professors we would quote: A. Humbert, **Essai d'une théologie du scandale dans les synoptiques:** Biblica 35 (1954) 1-28; **La morale de S. Paul: Morale du plan du salut. Essai d' une théologie morale dans les épîtres pauliniennes adressées à des communautés:** Mélanges Sc. Rel. 15 (1958) 5-44; R. Koch, **Geist und Messias. Ein Beitrag zur Theologie des Alten Testamentes,** Vienna, 1950; **Die Wertung des Besitzes im Lukasevangelium:** Biblica 38 (1957) 151-169; **Témoignage d'après les Actes:** Masses Ouvrière n. 129 (1957) 16-33; n. 131 (1957) 4-25; **Erlösungstheologie Genesis 1-11** (Theologische Brennpunkte, vol. 1), Bergen-Enkheim, 1965.

incredibly rapid change in the structures and conditions of life, we need to distinguish very clearly between what is changeable and what is not in our own tradition. This is hardly possible if we only know the moral theology of yesterday. It is getting to be generally admitted that the moral theologians most faithful to tradition are not those who continue uncritically and without change to follow the stereotyped *Institutiones theologiae moralis* such as they have developed in the seventeenth century.[4]

The whole rich tradition, from the Fathers to our own time, must be used for the renewal of moral theology. The Fathers are particularly important in this connection; for we can and must learn from the great pastoral theologians of the early Church how to effectively present the originality and newness of Christian ethics in a non-Christian world with quite different moral views. Here the Greek Fathers are of special importance, not only because they were nearest to New Testament revelation both in time and in language, but especially also with regard to the return of Eastern Christendom to the one Church. The Eastern Christians will find the invitation to reunion all the more acceptable, the more they find that their rich inheritance is also alive with us[5] G. Teichtweier's comprehensive study of Origen's moral theology is an excellent example.[6] Lately much research has been done in

---

4. Cf. Bernard Häring, C.Ss.R., **The Law of Christ**, 3 vols. (Westminster, Md., Newman, 1961-1966), Foreword of Vol. I.

5. The insufficient knowledge of Greek on the part of many of our younger theologians is a great obstacle in this respect.

6. G. Teichtweier, **Die Sündenlehre des Origenes**, Regensburg, 1958. Cf. also, H. Huber, **Geist und Buchstabe der Sonntagsruhe, Eine historisch-theologische Untersuchung über das Verbot der knechtlichen Arbeit von der Urkirche bis auf Thomas von Aquin**, Salzburg, 1958. This

medieval and modern theology,[7] though even here much remains to be done. There has been a tendency lately to condemn everything in the moral theology of the last centuries as barren. Those studies that examine the function of moral theology in the context of its time, however, are tending to do it more justice concluding that moral theology has, in many ways, produced lasting results.[8]

It is precisely an unprejudiced view of the whole of tradition that makes it impossible for contemporary moral theologians to simply take over the system of one of their great predecessors, even of a giant like St. Thomas Aquinas. The teachings of the great men of the past are of permanent value; but it is not the least part of their greatness that they were consciously involved in the intellectual discussions of their time. The linguistic expression of their ideas bears the unmistakable hallmark of their time, that is to say their exact meaning can be understood only if the historical setting of the speaker and his partners in the discussion is taken into consideration. Their systems express the task of their time, namely to present the supra-temporal truth of salvation to their contemporaries in a manner that will attract them and show them how their concerns fit in the plan of salvation. Hence we are truly faithful to Augustine, Thomas, or Alphonsus Liguori

---

is an excellent study which deserves to be named as an example of the fruitfulness of historical research for systematic moral theology.

7. Among others we should like to mention the many individual studies by P. Delhaye and L. Vereecke (detailed bibliography in my book, **The Law of Christ, I,** pp 53-59).

8. Cf. my contributions: **La teologia morale cattolica in rapporto allo spirito dei tempi,** in Humanitas (Brescia) 13 (1958) 338-348. **Moraltheologie gestern und heute,** in Stimmen der Zeit 167 (1960) 99-110.

only if, like them, we sacrifice nothing of eternal truth; but also if, again like them, we tackle courageously the topical questions of our time[9] and deal with them in contemporary language, that is to say in a serious dialogue with the men and the intellectual tendencies of our time.

The great teachers of the past can be wronged in two ways: first, if their achievements are judged from the point of view of our times, instead of their own; secondly, if one single system is followed which reproduces exactly the formulae and ready-made casuistic solutions of a single master, while all other schools or new methods are despised or even attacked. In such a case intellectual sloth and narrowness are taken for faithfulness, even faithfulness to those great thinkers whose whole work was characterized by awareness of the needs of their time. True faithfulness to the gospel and to the spirit of the great doctors of the Church is possible only in truly Catholic comprehensiveness and humble courage to independence, as well as in the conscious will to do justice to the task before us.

Hence an "Alphonsian" moral theology — to name an example especially near to us — will take care not to continue the disputes of the eighteenth century which Alphonsus himself hated so much or to concentrate on its problems. It will even less attempt to apply mechanically to our own very different situation the casuistic solutions which Alphonsus had worked out with great good sense for the citizens and the neglected shepherds of the feudal society of the kingdom of Naples. Alphonsus approached the — also pastorally — burning dispute between rigorism (Jansenism, tutiorism) and laxism

---

9. Here we would mention especially W. Schöllgen, **Aktuelle Moral-probleme**, Düsseldorf, 1955; **Konkrete Ethik**, ibid., 1961.

and the question of the relationship between law and freedom in a way suitable for his time. It would be foolish to cast him aside, only because the problems of his time are not ours. This would be a misunderstanding of tradition in the same way as would be the attempt to claim the authority of some giant of the past for dispensing with any new theological effort or even for holding in suspicion any new expression of the moral teaching of the Church.

The theological tradition of the Church should not conjure up images of a peaceful graveyard with guards before dogmatic formulae written in a dead language,[10] but should rather make one think of the continuity of life in the spirit of the risen Christ. Obedience to the Spirit which he has sent us decides how vital and living this tradition will be.

Moral theologians must always warn Christians against the "spirit of the world," according to the words of St. Paul, "Do not be conformed to this world" (Rom 12:2). But they must also examine their own conscience and ask themselves whether all their theses, opinions and methods really correspond to the spirit of the gospel. On the other hand, the actual task of moral theology can not be accomplished unless we clearly distinguish between the "spirit of the world" and the "spirit of the time" (*Weltgeist* and *Zeitgeist*).

The "spirit of the world" is the mind and thought of unredeemed man, or, more exactly, the egocentric and supercilious way of the world, insofar as it clings to its darkness, despising the redeeming light of Christ.

---

10. For Thomas Aquinas and the medieval Schoolmen Latin was not a dead language. It is the fault of the humanists to have turned Latin into a dead language by rigorously imposing the norms of the ancient classical authors. Even today it can come alive in the hands of a powerful linguist, but only for those who know it perfectly.

On the other hand, "According to J. G. Herder (d. 1803), 'Zeitgeist' is defined as the universal expression of opinions, will and feelings forming the thought and life of men in a given historical period. It is one of the most potent sociological influences."[11] Thus understood the spirit of the time is neither pure light nor pure darkness. It not only has its dangers, but it also presents positive opportunities. If we believe in the Lord of history and the relation of all history to salvation history, then moral theologians must lovingly understand their contemporaries and must also eagerly try to perceive their genuine concerns as expressed in the spirit of the times. If these are given a positive place in theology and pastoral care we will be assisting in the redemption of the spirit of our time.

There are legitimate mutual relations between moral theologians and the spirit of the times. Through the ministry of the Church, including moral theology, the word of God is equally near to every period of time and always topical because of the action of the Spirit of God. This implies a rejection of all fundamentalism, according to which the literal repetition of biblical statements suffices, and which regards any new attempt at a theological systematization as superfluous. It is even more a rejection of the view of those who do not consider the Scriptures, but the work of some great doctor of the Church, as the final presentation of the saving message valid for all times and civilizations.

Truth is supra-temporal, this is an undoubted fact. But, as long as man has not reached his final destiny, the expression of truth and the means of knowing it are necessarily temporal and to a certain degree also conditioned by time. If theolo-

---

11. V. Schurr, **Religion und Zeitgeist,** in B. Häring, **Macht und Ohnmacht der Religion,** Salzburg, 1957, 317.

gians by-pass the concerns and language of their time in splendid isolation, pastors will undoubtedly do the same. The result will be that the spirit of our day will not be redeemed, but will become a prey to the dark powers of the "spirit of the world." A merely negative, wholesale "apologetic" rejection of the spirit of the times with the partly fossilized formulas of a theology beholden to a more or less distant past, is a scandal endangering salvation, which will provoke the spirit of the time to undesirable reaction, perhaps even to serious degeneration.

Guided by the magisterium, moral theologians should help the fermenting spirit of the time which desires clarity with their own deep and living faith; for the more they meet it in this way, the less danger will there be that they themselves unconsciously become its victims. We ought humbly to ask whether, in view of the powerful intellectual movements of our time, we ourselves do not share the guilt for certain wrong developments, and why these movements do not appear in purified form among Christians who are faithful to the Church. For the more we ask such questions, the more easily shall we discover just those truths of our faith which are most needed by our time and can express it most effectively.

In my opinion a constructive encounter with the spirit of our time demands a closer connection between moral and dogmatic theology, a clearer distinction from canon law, a greater influence of sociology and an integration of the principal themes and viewpoints of ascetical and mystical theology.

The most serious crisis of moral theology is connected with its constitution as a discipline of its own, that is with its being detached from an undivided theology. As a "practical discipline" it has become too closely attached to positive law, thus partly losing not only its necessary connection with Scripture, but also with systematic theology which, after its separation from moral theology, was called "dogmatic." It is one of the most important events in the present history of theology that the two branches of dogmatic and moral theology are once more moving towards each other,[12] though it is not yet quite clear how they will finally be divided or united in a new synthesis.

Owing to the liturgical and biblical renewal today the mystery of salvation has again moved into the center of dogmatic theology after having been rather neglected in the recent past. Dogmatic theologians are thinking more consciously in terms of salvation history, and thus the tremendous influence of the saving truth on the moral life of the Christian becomes more evident.

For the same reason of biblical and liturgical renewal, contemporary moral theologians also realize that the basis of moral theology cannot be the moral imperative as such, but the mystery of salvation from which all moral impulses derive. Hence, for the last twenty-five years, they have been constantly demanding that the whole of moral theology should be based more clearly and convincingly on dogma.[13] Characteristically Christian life can be described only as "speaking the truth in love . . . to grow up in every way into him who is the head, into Christ" (Eph 4:15).

Moral theology depends on the same sources as dogmatic

---

12. The most important dogmatic theologians moving in this direction are Karl Rahner and Michael Schmaus.

13. Cf. P. Delhaye, **Dogme et Morale, Autonomie et assistance mutuelle**: Mélanges Sc. Rel. 11 (1954) 49-62; **La théologie morale d'hier et d'aujourd' hui**: Melanges Sc. Rel. (1953) 112-130. Extensive bibliography in **The Law of Christ**, I, pp. 213-223.

theology, their methods are fundamentally the same. However, as long as moral theology is a special branch beside dogmatic theology, it can leave to the latter the doctrinal proof of all those truths that do not directly belong to it. Moral theologians, on the other hand, must bring out the dynamic character of the truths of revelation and, basing themselves on dogma, work out the theological synthesis that is concerned with life.

Though there are important inner connections between morality and law, the former does not derive from law as its true source. Such an assertion could only spring from the most one-sided legal positivism. Nor can positive law, whether civil or canon law, be the source, or at least the principal source, of moral theology, even though valid law includes a moral obligation, and the many unnecessary and unjust laws of our era demand a moral discussion.

After civil and canon law have become special branches of scholarship, it cannot be the duty of modern Catholic moral theologians to discuss the contents of ecclesiastical and secular laws. This would normally also be outside the competence of moral theologians, who have to know so many other things. On the other hand, they are bound thoroughly to discuss the moral obligation of human laws and to integrate obedience to ecclesiastical and secular authority with the New Testament "law of grace and love," elucidating it by typical examples. It must be shown in what spirit and according to which standards the Christian is to deal with human laws. Hence the moral theologian is concerned with interpreting the law according to the principles of morality.

We often hear the not quite unjustified complaint that the scientific moral theology of the last three centuries has not always escaped the danger of exaggerated legalism. What does this mean? A moral theology is "legalistic" if its presentation and subject matter neglect "the law of the Spirit of life in Christ Jesus" (Rom 8:2) in favor of a multiplicity of legal norms, especially if man's relation to God is misunderstood after the manner of human law.

We should like to illustrate the problem by some examples: a moral textbook treats on more than twenty pages all possible cases with regard to the ecclesiastical law of the eucharistic fast, but mentions only in passing in what state of mind Catholics should participate in Holy Mass, "fulfill their Sunday duty" and receive the Body of the Lord. It is not mentioned at all that the whole Christian life receives its inner dynamic of grace from the Eucharist. Another example. A moral textbook distinguishes with incredible accuracy between the strictly forbidden knitting and the permitted embroidering when treating of the Church's commandment of abstaining from servile work on Sunday. There is practically no distinction between what is a divine and what is a merely ecclesiastical commandment and what is only a casuistical addition of some moral theologian; and, even worse, the author of such books do not even consider it the duty of moral theology to treat of the deeper theological meaning of the Lord's day, of its liturgical importance and its relation to the resurrection of Christ. In a tradition of more than a thousand years sin is the true "servile work," but this type of morality regards it as quite indifferent whether this is committed on a Sunday or a weekday — Sunday seems to be only desecrated by legally forbidden manual labor. Even the treatment of the sacrament of penance is chiefly concerned with the way in which the material completeness of confession can be safeguarded and which punishments the priest may incur when administering it while hardly anything is said about the nature of conversion and its relation to the kingdom of God or about the liturgical praise of the justice and mercy of God in the celebration of the sacrament of penance. These aspects are left to the "ascetical literature," because they are not concerned with what can be legally defined.

It is the most palpable sign of exaggerated legalism if, like the practitioners of jurisprudence, moral theologians treat only of what can be defined by law, while leaving out the decisive question, whether the Christian as such should order his life only according to the minimum requirements of the general law, or if he must bear fruit according to the talents he has received. It is a departure from the spirit of the gospel to place the main emphasis on a minimum obligation imposed from outside, while treating the great Christian demands and the obligation involved in the gift of grace as of secondary importance. Hence we see the legalism of moral theology not so much in the preponderance of legal questions in the textbooks as rather in the confusion of purely legal and originally moral theological problems. We are, however, convinced that moral theology keeps itself free from juridical falsification much more easily if it leaves in principle the material treatment of all legal subject matter to canon law. Indeed, since the promulgation of the Codex Iuris Canonici such a development can be observed. We should leave the merely legal casuistry, which in some manuals of the last period covers up to nine tenths of the material, to the more competent canonists so that moral theology can remain free to deal with *moral-theological casuistics* which is usually treated much too cavalierly. Such casuistry ought to be quite clearly inspired by the essential laws of Christian morality, especially by the law of the solidarity of salvation, while nevertheless being in constant contact with contemporary life.

From the eighteenth century onwards, but especially since J. M. Sailer and J. B. Hirscher, the so-called "Germanic type" of Catholic moral theology (as against the Latin moral text books of the "Latin type") has always removed the merely legal matters. Here Tillmann has been most radical. In the last few decades the most vehement and often all too simplifying criticisms of legalism in morality have come especially from France.[14] But if there is too sudden a rupture we ought, in my opinion, to remain conscious of a considerable danger: though morality must not be made dependent on canon law, we must nevertheless be well aware of the inner relationship between "the law of the spirit of life in Christ Jesus" and the direction emanating from the pastoral office of the Church. If moral theologians do not carefully examine the relation between morality and law we shall arrive at a dangerous dichotomy, so that finally neither the canonists nor the pastors will be able to apply ecclesiastical law in a truly Christian spirit. Because of the very nature of the Church canon law needs to be consciously integrated into "the law of the spirit of life in Christ Jesus." In the *Decree on Priestly Formation* Vatican II offers a truly liberating perspective: "In the explanation of canon law ... the mystery of the Church should be kept in mind, as it was set forth in the *Dogmatic Constitution on the Church*, promulgated by this holy Synod" (No. 16).

---

14. E.g. B.J. Leclercq, **L'enseignement de la morale chrétienne**, Paris, 1950. His at times generalizing criticism applies only to a certain type of moral text books. The following two contributions are very informative: J. Leclercq, **Die neuen Gesichtspunkte unserer Zeit in der Erforschung der Moral**, and P. Delhaye, **Die gegenwärtigen Bestrebungen der Moralwissenschaft in Frankreich**, in V. Redlich (ed.), **Moralprobleme im Umbruch der Zeit**, Munich, 1957, 1-39.

In a relatively static period, positive law will apply to a large part of social life. The great social changes of the seventeenth and eighteenth centuries imprisoned moral theologians in so-called moral systems. The principal question they had to answer was this: "How far are undoubtedly valid positive laws of Church and state binding?" The laws in question were normally antiquated and no longer suited to the new situation, so that they began to stifle life. Though formal principles were of great importance in the solution of moral problems, the actual driving power was the virtue of prudence which took into account the nuances of the situation. Today we are experiencing much deeper and quicker changes. The problems they produce can no longer be solved by probabilism alone. We can no longer penetrate reality with one simple attentive glance; we need the help of modern empirical sociology. This is the science of the social entities, their changes and mutual relationships. It shows the differences between the formal (i.e. legal order) and the informal structure (i.e. the actual way of life). Now bureaucracy is slow, and the old generation often unduly conservative. The law is frequently only trying to catch up when life has already long passed it by. Hence the moral theologian should not be guided only by the positive law, especially in casuistics. This would be a sin against precisely the virtue of prudence which casuistry must serve.

Opinions may vary regarding the distinctions between moral, ascetical and mystical theology. But in recent times almost universal agreement has been reached on two principles: first, we ought not to give even the slightest cause for the idea that there are two moralities, one superior morality of the "works of supererogation" for religious and small elites of laymen, and a legal minimum morality for the masses. Though Catholic moralists never intended such a division, the methods of the *Institutiones theologiae moralis* of the last centuries and their differentiation from ascetical theology, together with certain unfortunate theses or expressions, have contributed considerably to arouse such a suspicion in our separated brethren. Even today we are often reproached for this, especially because the limited function of the "morality of the confessional" is not known in non-Catholic theological circles. Furthermore, it is objectively impossible to oppose ascetical theology as a doctrine of virtue to moral theology as a mere doctrine of duties; for in the morality of the New Testament the category of mere duty does not exist at all, even though it is important to distinguish between what can be imposed from outside as a duty by an earthly authority from what binds in one's inmost being by grace. On principle, duty as a Christian concept can be seen and presented only from the point of view of creation and grace. Christian morality is robbed of its inner dynamism and happiness if it is taught only as a complex of duties and definitions.[15]

Today moral theologians simply must boldly use sociology and social psychology; but this, of course, requires a clear distinction between legal statutes and the eternal principles of morality which must be integrated in the changed reality.

Today the empirical sociology of the family and pastoral sociology are undoubtedly of special importance.[16] For they show moral theologians the influence the social structures and

---

15. The important theologians of Tuebingen, Linsenmann and Schilling, followed by F. Tillmann, unfortunately still teach the division into three cycles of duties.

16. Cf. B. Häring, **The Sociology of the Family**, Cork, 1959; **Ehe in dieser Zeit**, Salzburg, 1964; **Macht und Ohnmacht der Religion**. Religionssoziologie als Anruf, Salzburg, 1957 (containing also a more detailed bibliography on the subject).

especially public opinion exercise on the religious and moral conduct of individuals and communities and vice versa, how ultimate ideals decide the change in structures and in public opinion. This will result in important knowledge in the sphere of casuistry and will also show how to effectively present the moral message of the Church to the men and women of our time.

Today moral theologians must make much greater use of all the social sciences than was necessary in past centuries, especially because of the tremendous power of the social forces at work in the world today. There is too much at stake for Christianity for us to neglect these important fields of study. Our social conscience must be better trained in casuistry.

Vatican II actually enjoins empirical pastoral sociology on the bishops as one of their duties: "In order to be able to consult more suitably the welfare of the faithful according to the condition of each one, a bishop should strive to become duly acquainted with their needs in the social circumstances in which they live. Hence, he ought to employ suitable methods, especially social research" (*Decree on the Bishops' Pastoral Office in the Church*, No. 16; cf. No. 17 and 22).

It is encouraging to note that the young generation of moral theologians shares with St. Paul the confidence that, far from being weakened by the "law of faith" (cf. Rom 3:31) and the "law of grace," the moral imperative is actually strengthened by them and placed in its true setting.

As opposed to the moralists of the age of rationalism a moral theologian must feel humiliated if he is turned into a mere frontier guard, while the subsidiary subject of ascetical and mystical theology is assigned all that is regarded as sublimely Christian. If moral theology is to be truly theology it must deal with the whole "law of perfection" (Jas 1:25) as is fitting our eschatological age. Its domain stretches from the limit of death, below which no one is allowed to fall, to the perfect realization of Christian existence to which all must tend. Above all it must show and make felt in all its treatises that the Christian life is a life of constant growth, an unremitting struggle for perfection.

But what, then, is left to ascetical theology? When moral theology confined itself mostly to the task of setting the confessor up as a "judge," ascetical theology became a separate supplementary science. If it is to continue as an independent subject, it might usefully present various ways of Christian living together with an appropriate historical and sociological background. As such it will be particularly valuable as a practical instruction on the art of using the various means to sanctity of life according to one's position, psychology and degree of perfection. We should prefer a more integrated approach, however, with ascetical-mystical, psychological-educational, speculative and, finally, casuistical methods all brought together into some kind of an organic synthesis.

For purposes of study, clarity and systematization are certainly needed. This does not mean, however, that we may limit ourselves to a mere notional theology and the presentation of material. Moral theologians are realizing again what ascetical-mystical theologians have never forgotten, namely that theology is by nature linked to existence, that it is essentially the engagement of faith. Hence the theological lecture, too, must be a testimony of faith, capable of involving and deepening the faith of the students. In other words, the method of theology, too, must be kerygmatic, the preaching of the mystery of salvation. Every true theology must be a theology of the heart. The intellectual realization, the *fides quaerens intellectum,* demands that the heart should be involved. This leads us to the question of content, and especially to the problem of approaches to the study of moral theology.

Catholic moral theology must be above all Christocentric. All exegetes agree that New Testament morality, like the preaching of the truth of salvation, is Christocentric through and through. Christ's message does not center in an abstract principle, but in his own Person. The love of the heavenly Father becomes visible and is experienced in him. "He who has seen me has seen the Father" (Jn 14:9). "In him we have redemption, the forgiveness of sins. He is the image of the invisible God, the first-born of all creation . . . all things were created through him and for him" (Col 1:14-16).

Christ redeems us from fateful anthropocentrism. The first Adam wanted to have some wisdom from himself; he wanted to reserve at least a small sphere of self-will to himself. The punishment was death. But Christ is "from the Father" (Jn 1:14); his whole being and his saving function are directed towards the Father, "to the glory of God the Father" (Phil 2:11). Christ never tires of emphasizing that he does not seek his own will and honor, but the will and the honor of the Father who has sent him. All his divine-human actions reveal his eternal nature of being the Word of the Father who gives himself back to his Father as undividedly as the Father expresses all his glory, love and wisdom in this his co-equal Word.

According to the clear statements of Scripture, and indeed its whole structure, there is no other way to the mystery of the Triune God than Christ. There are exponents of a certain "theology" who assert that a scholarly theology must not be built on Christ, because this would necessarily lead to an "anthropocentric theology"; but such theologians think in categories which are quite different from those of holy Scripture.[17]

The earliest Fathers of the Church[18] constantly emphasize that Christ himself is "the law and the covenant." He is the law of our life through the Holy Spirit whom he sends and who reflects his life in us.

We owe the magnificent beginnings of a systematic moral

---

17. B. Olivier, O.P., is of a different opinion. He writes in **Pour une théologie morale renouvelée** in **Morale Chrétienne et requêtes contemporaines**, Tournai-Paris, 1954, p. 250: "To want to construct a theology exclusively based on the fact of Christ is to destroy the very idea of theology; it is pretending to make, in reality, an anthropocentric theology — two contradictory terms. Without doubt, a Christocentric theology, and therefore centered, in fact, on human history, responds truly well to contemporary perspectives. A theology of this kind seems even to situate itself more correctly on the gospel. But this is only in appearance. . . . Beyond and independent of God's decision concerning creation and the human history, there is God in himself, in his eternal Trinitarian mystery. And it is this divine Reality which forms the point of departure for every authentic theology." Here the author seems to have forgotten that Christ is not only true man, but also true God, and that he is this in an hypostatic, indissoluble union. For the children of Adam, imprisoned in the anthropocentrism of original sin, there is no possibility to return to theocentrism without Christ. A Christocentric theology of salvation history is not based on merely human history, but on the history of God with man. In Christ and through Christ God's word to mankind is not only full of divine majesty, it is also the answer from human history, the answer of the head of mankind is the answer of the Son of God. The object of theology is not the Triune God in so far as, absolutely speaking, he need not have revealed himself; for if he had not done so, there would be no men and no theology. The theology of man is essentially and radically concerned with the saving truth, with God, the Father of our Lord Jesus Christ, with the God who reveals himself to us.

18. This fact is attested by many references, e.g. in J. Daniélou, **Théologie du Judéo-Christianisme**, Tournai, 1958, 216-19.

theology to Clement of Alexandria (d. before 216), whose great concern was to base morality wholly on Christ. Following Paul, he regarded the Old Testament Law as the "pedagogue leading to Christ." He further affirmed that all true moral knowledge including that of the pagans is ultimately "seeds scattered by the Logos." The ethical insights of the philosophers, and quite generally reason and the natural law (*lex naturae*), belong to Christian moral doctrine because and insofar as everything has been created in the Person of the Word of the Father all is directed towards Christ.

The Fathers did not yet visualize moral theology as a special branch of theology. Their theology was intimately linked with the pastoral office of the actual theologians, that is to say the bishops. Thus the preaching of the moral message was perfectly united to the message of salvation, and this in its turn with the celebration of the saving mysteries. Hence, it was quite natural for them to regard Christ himself as the norm, the center and the goal of the Christian life, who was at the same time the way to the Father, truth in person, life and the giver of life (cf. Jn 14:6). They did not only think of Christ as the Jesus of history, such as he showed himself by word and example in his earthly life. No, he is above all the only Son, generated by the Father before time began, born of the virgin Mary in the fullness of time, suffered and died, rose again from the tomb and ascended into heaven, whence Christendom expects him to come with infinite longing, so that his work may be completed. He stands before them as the living Christ who continues to live and work in his Church and its holy mysteries and thus communicates his law together with his life and grace.

Some scholars hold that the first great system of moral

theology, namely the second part of the Summa theologica of St. Thomas Aquinas, marks the end of the Christocentric moral doctrine of the "pre-scientific" (*vorwissenschaftlich*) period. Much could be said in reply to this. St. Thomas himself did not mean to produce a self-contained presentation of moral doctrine; like all his great predecessors he knew only the one undivided theology, the center of which was the doctrine of Christ. The all-embracing core of his theology is not the somewhat Aristotelian idea of beatitude, which introduces the *Prima Secundae* of the *Summa*, but the doctrine of God, the Creator and Perfecter of all things, who has revealed himself in Jesus Christ, our Redeemer, in whom we possess the image of God and in whom we are given the love of the Father. The *Summa* is arranged as follows: Man in the Word of God, created in God's image (*Pars Prima*), called by grace freely to show forth the divine image (*Pars Secunda*), finds the only way to his goal in Jesus Christ (*Pars Tertia*). We should like to emphasize that the theology of St. Thomas is thoroughly Christocentric. Christology together with the doctrine of the sacraments is the great finale of this grandiose work. Nevertheless, it cannot be denied that later separate development of moral theology were adversely affected by St. Thomas' treatment of the majority of moral themes in the *Pars Secunda*, hence before Christology and the doctrine of the sacraments. It was still absolutely clear to Thomas that man as such cannot be discussed without Christ, but this was later forgotten.

When Catholic moral theology became independent, its essentially Christocentric aspect was temporarily neglected, even though hardly denied. The reason for this is above all its limited end: while in the early Middle Ages the *Libri*

Paenitentiales gave practical help to determine penances in confession, from the thirteenth century manuals for confessors, called *Summae Confessariorum* came into use as a kind of encyclopedia for the various questions arising from the administration of the sacrament of penance. At the time of the Counter Reformation, after the Council of Trent, the sacrament of penance came to be of greater practical importance, and the Jesuits especially were actively concerned with a more thorough training of the mostly uneducated confessors. Thus casuistry became a special subject in the *ratio studiorum* of the Society, being furnished with an absolute minimum of principles for adequately solving cases of conscience, while the actual theology of the Christian life was reserved to the main subject of theology. When the limited viewpoint of casuistry became increasingly independent it gave itself the high-sounding name of "moral theology" (*Institutiones theologiae moralis*), while dogmatic theologians dispensed themselves more and more from treating the moral aspect of the doctrine of faith. In this development the anti-Protestant notion of "fides credenda" (the faith that must be believed) probably played a considerable part.

From all of this we can see how the constitution of moral theology as a separate subject was considerably influenced by the period in which it took place and by the needs of those times. In view of the importance of the spiritual director at that time the result was a useful recipe for solving questions of conscience and judging the penitent. All this was a part of pastoral theology, to which some more general principles were added later.

Moral theology proper, that is the doctrine of the essence

of Christian living, had become increasingly the concern of ascetical-mystical literature and preaching, where the Christocentric aspect was somehow preserved.[19]

The type of "moral theology" which had been developed in the seventeenth century remained almost uncontested until the twentieth century, at least in the Latin countries; but today it is often condemned precisely because it is not Christocentric. To be just, however, we ought not only consider its limited goal but also its historical background: at a time when most Europeans were still conscious of Christ as the way, the truth and the life and in which the unity of the whole of theology had still been preserved, the *Institutiones theologiae moralis* could probably still be tolerated. Today, however, it can no longer be countenanced because in our urgent struggle against laicism we must emphasize particularly the specifically Christian elements, and in a pluralistic society we must oppose the truly Christian characteristics and the glorious witness of an authentic Christian life to the multitude of other moral systems.

Despite many voices calling for change, moral theologians did not do their duty in time, hence in the last hundred years Catholic ascetical literature and preaching, too, degenerated into a shallow moralism, which was doubly dangerous in an era of militant secularism. However, there have always been efforts to produce a Christocentric moral theology. Beginning

---

19. We might remember the teaching about the truly Christian life in the Order of St. Ignatius of Loyola, in St. Francis de Sales and especially in the École Française of the seventeenth century, as well as in the writings of Cardinal Bérulle, Condren, Jean Eudes, and Bossuet, who considered the Christian life essentially from the point of view of the interior assimilation to Christ, priest and victim. Cf. J. Gautier, **Some Schools of Catholic Spirituality**, New York, 1959.

with J. M. Sailer and J. B. Hirscher and continuing with Magnus Jocham and Fritz Tillmann, these efforts have become steadily more effective and far-reaching.[20]

In the age of Vatican II Christocentric moral theology is based especially on the Pauline "being in Christ." "The law of Christ" (Gal 6:2) is "the law of the Spirit of life in Christ Jesus" (Rom 8:2), through which we can love the heavenly Father and all members of the Body of Christ, indeed all mankind that needs to be saved, through Christ's Spirit with Christ's own love.

We cannot imitate Christ externally, since many of his actions are bound up with his own unique Person. We can live in Christ Jesus through the gift of grace, from which follows the "imitation" as the freely given obedience to his person, his word and his example. The law which completely binds us to Christ is ultimately the grace of the Holy Spirit which is poured out in our hearts and wants to make us Christ-like. This view derives from the teaching of St. Thomas, the faithful witness of tradition: "The essential thing in the law of the New Covenant, and in which its whole power consists, is the grace of the Holy Spirit, which is given by the faith in Christ. And thus the new law is principally the very grace of the Holy Spirit." The external law, transmitted to us in the written and spoken word, is mentioned only in the second place, which does not mean, however, that it is unimportant, if it shares in the vitality of the inner law: "It disposes to the grace of the Holy Spirit and to the right use of this grace" (S. Th. I/II^{ae}, q. 106 a. 1).

---

20. On the history of modern moral theology, cf. my book. **The Law of Christ**, I, pp. 22-33.

Hence in our view it is one of the basic tasks of contemporary moral theologians to show how all religious and moral demands, including those of the natural law and the positive laws, must be understood in the context of the life-giving love of Christ; more, they must lead to a very personal relation to Christ and to a docility to the Christ-given Spirit which should go far beyond what is, or can be, expressed in the form of law.[21]

The grace of the Holy Spirit, which gives us a share in the law of Christ, has its center in the holy sacraments. In them the saving mysteries of the Word made man act on us most effectively. A Christocentric moral theology characterized by the paschal mystery of the death and resurrection of Christ is in all its parts a "sacramental" moral theology.

The theology and preaching of the Fathers was wholly the kerygma of the mystery of salvation. Instruction on the Christian life was chiefly given in connection with the sacramental teaching and during the celebration of the liturgy, always with a view to the saving mystery of Christ's death and resurrection. Thus the new experience of Christian moral teaching resulted directly from the newness of the life that had been received in the sacrament.

The mystagogical catecheses of Cyril of Jerusalem (d. 386, or, in the opinion of many contemporary patrologists, of John of Jerusalem) are a classical example. The medieval Schoolmen, too, more or less subscribed to this view of things. The moral treatises of an undivided theology are usually connected with the saving truths of creation and incarnation and particularly with the doctrine of the sacraments. Even though

---

21. Cf. **The Law of Christ**, I, pp. 252-263.

Thomas Aquinas sometimes followed new ways of thought, he treats a large part of moral doctrine within the doctrine of the sacraments in the Third Part of the *Summa*.

Only in the modern *Institutiones theologiae moralis* were the sacraments treated as added "duties" after the commandments of the Law of Sinai, with special emphasis on their legal aspects. It is hardly mentioned any more that, because the sacraments give us new life in Christ, they also involve the duty to live in the spirit of Christ. We might well say with slight exaggeration: the more moralists treat of the sacraments only with regard to the legal requirements of their administration and reception, the more closely does their description of moral commandments and duties approach secular ethics.

The liturgical renewal has once more placed the mystery of Christ at the center of Christian life. The powerful eucharistic-liturgical movement which started with St. Pius X has thankfully not degenerated into mere aestheticism or formalism, as had been asserted by some of its moralistic critics. True, it took its time until its thrust had transformed itself also into moral impulses. But today it has already become clear that the liturgy is once more the center and source of a truly supernatural life and that the apostolate of the whole people of God derives its impetus from the altar.[22] Current day modernism had been nourished on anthropocentric humanism and rationalism; it has now received its death blow, even though at first only by the élite who gladly welcomed the

---

22. These statements are founded on empirical research. Cf. B. Häring, **Die gemeinschaftsstiftende Kraft der Liturgie:** Liturgisches Jahrbuch 7 (1957) 205-214; **L'importance communautaire des sacrements dans l'Eglise:** Lumen Vitae 13 (1958) 446-454.

pentecostal spring of a renewed and vitalized liturgy. Owing to the Council this attitude is now shared by the whole people of God (cf. *The Constitution on the Liturgy* and *Lumen gentium*).

Moral theologians cannot by-pass this evident action of the Holy Spirit in the Church of today. The new generation has been formed by this spirit from the beginning. A theologian like Fritz Tillmann who has otherwise done so much for the renewal of moral theology could still entitle his presentation of the sacraments "Duties towards oneself in the religious realm."[23] But today the whole of moral theology is seen under the aspect of its sacramental structure: the sacraments are regarded as the decisive elements in the building up of the people of God, which is wholly devoted to the praise of God, the apostolate of love and the sanctification of the world. The active participation of the laity in the apostolate of the Church receives powerful impetus from a deeper understanding of the social aspects of baptism, confirmation, matrimony and sacred orders, but most of all from the experience of their communion in Christ, given and testified by the Eucharist. We can, for example, meet the much discussed "crisis of the sacrament of penance" by laying less emphasis on the penitent's own effort and more on his personal encounter with the crucified, risen and judging Christ and by viewing man's cooperation from this angle, as well as from the social point of view.

Todays moral theologians must honestly admit that such a view of the Christian life in our age has not been prepared and popularized by their own department of knowledge,

---

23. Not only here, but particularly on this point, my own views differ considerably from those of Tillmann.

though this would actually have been competent to do so. On the contrary, the exponents of systematic moral theology have been compelled by the spontaneous general revival of this ancient view to compare their own teaching with it and make up for what they have neglected. By integrating this deeper view with the apostolic kerygma and patristic theology, they will help to assist the rise of new ideas, preserve the liturgical movement from one-sided "liturgism" and overcome moralism.

Catholic moral doctrine remains, of course, a doctrine of norms but apart from all individual norms we shall once more become more conscious of the fact that the Holy Spirit gives us the innermost principle and the goal of the life in Christ in the sacraments and in the saving mysteries of the incarnate Word.

In sacramental piety and life a double aspect of the biblical message of the kingdom of God established by Christ is clearly expressed; first, that it is a reign of grace, secondly, that the rule of divine love founds and demands by its very essence a kingdom of love. In this interim period between the coming of the Spirit and the Parousia, Christ meets us personally in the sacraments, placing us in the kingdom of his saving love and preparing us for his coming. Thus, through their fullness of grace, the sacraments are a constant preaching of the divine imperative of this "last hour." The gifts we receive very personally attach us sensibly to the mystery of the Body of Christ. By thus saying Yes to grace as to the true norm we also agree to the common apostolate, in which we fulfill our special function in the saved community.

The eucharistic movement under St. Pius X was followed by the beginning of the lay apostolate under Pius XI and Pius XII. Thus the sacraments were experienced as continually active saving powers of the kingdom of God, and their social function was expressed also in the form of their celebration; it followed from this that there came into being also a new consciousness of the nature of the Church. Moral theologians of the past had visualized the individual Christain mainly as an obedient subject of the hierarchically governed Church, whereas today he is seen above all as a co-responsible member of the people of God. Thus obedience, too, acquires a new motive. It sometimes seemed as if liturgical piety and apostolate were in hostile competition with each other. This, however, was a mistaken view of both realities and their true relationship. It emerges clearly in the Church of today that the mysteries of the New Law are the dynamic forces that build up the kingdom of God and that their inspired celebration produces a powerful impulse for the apostolate of both priests and laity, proceeding from the experience of the saving mysteries.

The perspectives of moral theology have also been broadened by social theology and social ethics, which came to play a greater part ever since the time of Leo XIII.

Today moral theologians begin to present the fundamental principles for pastoral care (*Umweltseelsorge*)[24] as deriving from the saving mystery and the essentially social nature of man. As the Christian is essentially a member of the saved community built up round the altar, so his affirmation of God's kingdom and his moral life are realized not in isolation and separation, but in his personal solidarity with his surroundings and his manifold relations with them. The theology of the milieu[25] in the framework of the doctrine of the Kingdom of

---

24. Cf. V. Schurr, **Seelsorge in einer neuen Welt,** Salzburg, 1959; **Konstruktive Seelsorge,** Freiburg, 1962.
25. Cf. V. Schurr, **Theologie der Umwelt,** in "Theologie in Geschichte

God confronts systematic moral theology with many new
tasks, which have been energetically approached in many individual studies, especially about a theology of the laity and
the earthly realities.[26]

The goal of moral effort is not only the salvation of the
individual. The very structure of moral theology must make
it clear that the glorification of God, the social fullness and
solidarity of redemption and individual salvation form a single
entity. The entire cosmos has been redeemed and we must
gain the whole world for Christ. Thus the ethical sphere with
its norms and motivations is becoming much larger than the
old morality, which is still mainly concerned with individual
salvation alone.

The doctrine of the last things is no longer used only to
frighten the sinner: The expectation of the Lord and the
consummation of all things are motives of hope for the
Christian community and at the same time act as a spur to
Christianize all spheres of existence. This was frequently em-
phasized by the *Pastoral Constitution of the Church in the
Modern World* (see also the *Dogmatic Constitution on the
Church,* ch. 7).

Catholic moral theologians ought not present the moral
life as a series of minutely detailed obligations and prohibi-
tions; for the New Testament law of life is essentially something other than a law imposed from outside. It is rather a law
of grace urging us from within, served by the external law

---

und Gegenwart" (Michael Schmaus zum 60. Geburtstag, Munich, 1956,
145-180. Cf. also my book, **Ehe in dieser Zeit,** Salzburg, 1960. The
Council, especially its **Pastoral Constitution on the Church in the Modern
World,** will probably have a decisive influence on this subject.

26. Esp. Yves Congar, Gustave Thiles, Gérard Philips, Alfons Auer.

in its directing and accusing functions. In the view of St. Paul the moral and religious life of the Christian is determined by God's action as a force and a power (*dynamis, kratos*) revealing itself as the glorious love of God. "The love of Christ controls us" (2 Cor 5:14). The mysteries of the death and resurrection of Christ are working in the "power of the Holy Spirit" (cf. Acts 1:8) in order to assimilate us ever more closely to the image of Christ.

Christian morality cannot be identified with a merely static law of minimum requirements, as the *Institutiones theologiae moralis* sometimes seemed to suggest, nor does it correspond to the Stoic ideal of virtue either, according to which "one either has virtue perfectly or not at all." During his pilgrim's state here on earth the Christian must always realize that he is not yet perfect, that he is still in a state of becoming. Life under the law of grace is essentially also under the law of growth. For to him who uses his talent well "more will be given" (Mk 13:12; Lk 19:26). But if a man refuses to progress according to the grace given to him, he will also lose his one talent. This truth is classically expressed by St. Paul: "Not that I have already obtained this or am already perfect; but I press on to make it my own, because Christ Jesus has made me his own. Brethren, I do not consider that I have made it my own." This is followed by a specific address to the *teleioi*, the eschatological men and women, who are obliged to be perfect, but who do not think themselves perfect like the Stoics: "Let those of us who are mature (in German: perfect) be thus minded" (Phil 3:12-15).

In accordance with biblical and patristic thought this point of view must once more be emphasized more strongly today. In the last century Sailer, Hirscher, Deutinger, Werner, Fuchs, Jocham and Linsenmann especially have stressed this psychological and dynamic view in their manuals of moral theology; hence they have emphasized especially the doctrine of the law of grace (of the talents), the working of the Holy Spirit, the freedom of the children of God and man's docility to every grace.

The Christian must always carry the burden of Adam; therefore in the time of eschatological separation and decision, the law of growth means for him constant conversion, constant struggle and self-denial. It does not suffice to restrict the doctrine of conversion to a special treatise, for the whole presentation of Catholic moral theology must be marked by it. To cite only one example: mortal and venial sin may not be defined purely and statically by the object; the personal factor must be accorded decisive consideration, together with the law of growth and constant conversion. Hence the distinction of sins "ex genere" (gravely or venially sinful) and "ex toto genere" may only be regarded as indicative.[27] Moral knowledge, moral freedom, and even the tenderness and sincerity of the conscience must be presented in the light of man's eschatological obligation to become ever more perfect.

The disciple of Christ must grow through the grace given him "to the measure of the stature of the fullness of Christ" (Eph 4:13). This is something quite other than the Aristotelian idea of self-perfection. The Christian law of growth receives its true dynamism not from the "eros," that is from man's self-centered striving for perfection and happiness. The decisive force which directs man to the greater glory of God and his own perfection is "God's love (which) has been poured into our hearts through the Holy Spirit," the echatolog-

---

27. Cf. F. Böckle, **Bestrebungen in der Moraltheologie: Fragen der Theologie heute** (ed. J. Feiner et al.), Einsiedeln, 1957, 434f.

ical fullness of salvation.[28] Now the love of Christ which urges us is echoed in the natural longing of the human heart which is raised up by the virtue of hope. But while the false personalism of humanistic perfectionism follows too closely the anthropocentric line of the first Adam, biblical personalism can be understood only through Christ, who has redeemed us to a theocentric life.

The heart of Christian personalism is the agape, the love that gives man a share in the relationship of the three divine Persons.[29] The creative call of God constitutes us as persons, it calls us by our name and enables us to answer. Our personality is raised to a higher plane through Christ, who is the Word of the Father and the valid answer in the name of all humanity. Through the working of the Holy Spirit we have received in Christ a new name from the Father, so that we can now answer as children: "Abba, Father." We become mature personalities by being open to the inner urge and call of God's love and answer, like Christ, by the serving love of our neighbor. For Christian personalism love is not a mere commandment, even less one that would come to man from outside: the love we receive from God is fundamental to Christian personality and existence. What we are as Christians, we are through the love of God. The great commandment of love is the decisive expression of our new life.

Because of its own essence and our being in Christ the great commandment of the love of God and our neighbor

---

28. The call for perfection (to be **teleios**) derives from the fullness of grace of the last times (**telos**) which force a decision and look to the second coming of Christ. Cf. H. Preisker, **Das Ethos des Urchristentums,** Gütersloh, 1949.

29. Cf. The chapter "Inner Unity of Divine Love" in my book **The Law of Christ,** II, 351ff.

points to the Holy Spirit, the pentecostal gift of Christ, sitting on the right hand of the Father. The New Testament law is summed up in our submission to the Holy Spirit, being led by him is the true expression of Christian personalism. This implies also the importance of the gifts of the Holy Spirit in a moral theology centered in the theological virtue of charity. It does not suffice to assign a gift of the Holy Spirit to each virtue, this would be artificial. But all parts of moral theology ought to show that the true disciple of Christ is characterized by docility to the grace of the Holy Spirit, which likens our attitude to the loving surrender of Christ.

According to the neo-pagan existentialism of Sartre, for example, the dignity and freedom of man is endangered by an absolutely valid moral law. Wanting to be a demiurge of his own existence and its meaning, he establishes an order of values according to his own plan;[30] even more: without subscribing to any definite hierarchy of values, he wants to prove his own freedom (or better, his own glory) again and again.

Against such an existentialism and the anti-law situation ethics derived from it, Catholic theologians must now emphasize especially the unchangeable moral law and also distinguish it clearly from antinomian currents of present-day Protestantism which is made even more dangerous by modern situation ethics.[31] But for this precise reason we must dis-

---

30. The ethical system of Nikolai Hartmann is typical of this attitude, though he is not yet an existentialist in the sense of Sartre.

31. A typical representative of an antinomian Protestant situation ethic is e.g. K. Barth, **Die kirchliche Dogmatik, III**, 4, Zollikon-Zürich, 1951. After profound discussions of what makes adultery, remarriage after divorce, suicide, abortion and many other things a sin, he repeats monotonously that this cannot be understood in the sense of Catholic legalism. Thus, in certain situations the Christian would be justified or

sociate ourselves from those obstinate Catholic adaptations of situation ethics which are late derivations of nominalism and legal positivism, and according to which we apparently ought to literally fulfill the positive law even if by doing so we offend against the natural moral law or against the gospel order of grace.[32] We shall not be able to convince an existentialist that even the most urgent situation does not allow us to go against the essential order, even though this may be done with a good conscience by claiming a "legal situation" produced by the positive law.

But apart from clearly rejecting errors we must also bring to light the hidden and frequently falsified concern of modern existentialism, which does not only take the form of Sartre's philosophy. It finds so many adherents, because it has not always been given its rightful place in Christian life and theology. We are thinking of St. Paul's passionate struggle against dull, anthropocentric legalism, and of his positive teaching about the freedom of the children of God under the superabundant law of the Holy Spirit.

The wrong situation ethic wants to break up the law of the Creator and Redeemer which binds all in favor of the "works of the flesh." In practice it replaces the laws established by God and lawful human authority by the whims of self-will according to the "situation." Nevertheless, this also involves the serious desire to do justice to the many forms of life. In view of all this, contemporary Catholic theologians

---

even obliged to do the opposite, in obedience to his faith and after strict examination of his motives. This situation ethic may partly attributed to a lack of distinctions.

32. More in my essay: "Hartnaeckige Verwandte der Situationsethik," in **Theologie der Gegenwart** 4 (1961) 1-7.

will have to show that Christian living under the "law of grace" does not obey impersonal laws which are hostile to life, but the guidance of the life-giving Spirit and the Master who lovingly calls him. We ought also to show more clearly than the *Institutiones theologiae moralis* of the preceding centuries how the spiritual law of life in Christ Jesus is related to the instructions of the written law.

Thus a right understanding of the dynamic law of Christ's grace and love results in a personalism and existentialism which uncovers the miserable poverty of the humanist-anthropocentric "personalism" and expresses the longing of modern man for dignity and authenticity.

A scientific moral theology, therefore, can not and must not be a mere collection of individual laws, duties or norms, like a book of law. If it were merely this, it would not only betray its most sublime task, it would also hide the essence of Christian morality and destroy its inner dynamic. Since today so many departments of knowledge have lost their true center, it is the most important duty of moral theologians to work out the great leading ideas of their subject.

The points we have made in the preceding pages must, like all the tasks of moral theology, form a whole. Nevertheless, the way in which they are synthesized and the way in which various points of view are emphasized will change according to the spiritual outlook and temperament of individual theologians. The mystery of Christian morality is so rich that it can be fathomed only through a variety of attempts to systematize it. The Person of Christ, however, must always be at the center, and our relationship to him must become manifest in our sacramental assimilation to him and our adoring and obedient love for him and in him for the heavenly Father.

In other words: the Christian life must always be understood as the imitation of Christ, no matter whether we start with the concept of imitation or with another. We cannot, of course, derive all truths from the idea of imitation. Theology is never in the first place concerned with making deductions from a notion, but with humbly listening to every truth, though it will then also synthesize the fullness of truth that is given to us, insofar as it is possible for man.

2

THE MYSTERY OF THE CHURCH IN
THE MIRROR OF CHRISTIAN MORALITY

The introduction to the *Constitution on the Sacred Liturgy* of Vatican II says something important about the relation of the Christian life to the mystery of the Church: "The liturgy is the outstanding means by which the faithful can express in their lives, and manifest to others, the mystery of Christ and the real nature of the true Church."[1] This sentence is, as it were, the introit of the Council, at the center of which is the mystery of the Church, pointing clearly in the direction in which moral theology after the Second Vatican Council is to develop. Ecclesiology, in which the Church takes account of itself, must and will be reflected in the understanding of the Christian life. The more conscious this is, the more fruitful will the Council become for the life of the Church, of the faithful, and also for moral theology which, after all, must serve life.

We will now endeavor to work out the main lines of ecclesiology such as they emerge from the Council, and their parallels in the fundamental structure of Christian morals.

The ecclesiological theme of the Council appears already in the pentecostal message of 1960, in which Pope John XXIII expressed his hope for a new Pentecost, and where the Church is unmistakably seen in relation to Christ. At the same time it became clear that the Church was to be considered from the pastoral point of view, to be realized in the Christian life,

---

1. No. 2.

according to the unity of truth and love. After briefly mentioning that the Council demanded a profound grasp of the doctrinal principles from everyone, John XXIII continued: "The triumph of Jesus Christ is the ideal of all the redeemed. It is the ideal which every community, family, nation, and the whole universe, but particularly the holy, Catholic and apostolic Church must serve, and in whose service the Council, too, must be placed. We shall be on the road to true progress if Christ grows in us, because we are lovingly putting into practice the truths he taught. The stirring, mysterious words that the Apostle Paul addressed to the Ephesians ought to be written above the doors of the Ecumenical Council: "He, Christ, is the head from whom the whole body, joined and knit together by every joint with which it is supplied, when each part is working properly, derives its bodily growth and upbuilds itself in love' (Eph 4:15f). The radiant lines which form the beautiful and glorious image of the Catholic Church in the Ecumenical Council may easily be detected in the individual statements of the Pauline text. Truth and love: Christ, the summit and head of the mystical Body."[2]

Ecclesiology is essentially Christocentric. The Church can receive itself, its mystery and its mission only from Christ, and it can know them only through looking at Christ, at his mystery and mission. It can and must never be concerned with its own triumph, but always and everywhere only with the victory of the love of Christ. The Church must live the mystery of Christ in self-denial, in the vocation it has received, in the service of love and the praise of the triune God.

Christ was sent by the Father in order to reveal his love

---

2. **Discorsi, messagi, colloqui del Santo Padre Giovanni XXIII**, II, 396f; Cf. also Paul VI, **Ecclesiam suam** (Aug. 6, 1964).

effectively to men, to make it visible and capable of being experienced, and with the same love Christ sends his Church into the world. Its mission is to announce him, and through him the love of the Father in heaven, not only in rational categories, but with the splendor of his love which shines forth in truth, through the Church's witness, its unity and service. "When Jesus rose up again after suffering death on the cross for mankind, he manifested that he had been appointed Lord, Messiah, and Priest forever (cf. Acts 2:36); Heb 5:6; 7:17-21), and he poured out on his disciples the Spirit promised by the Father (cf. Acts 2:33). The Church, consequently, equipped with the gifts of her Founder and faithfully guarding his precepts of charity, humility, and self-sacrifice, receives the mission to proclaim and to establish among all peoples the kingdom of Christ and of God. She becomes on earth the initial budding forth of that kingdom. While she slowly grows, the Church strains toward the consummation of the kingdom and, with all her strength, hopes and desires to be united in glory with her King."[3]

The Council proves this fundamental concern in its very first message to the world: "Faith, hope and the love of Christ impel us to serve our brothers, thereby patterning ourselves after the example of the divine teacher, who 'came not to be served but to serve' (Mt 20:28). Hence the Church, too, was not born to dominate but to serve. He laid down his life for us, and we too ought to lay down our lives for our brothers (1 Jn 3:16)."

At the beginning of the second session of the Council Pope Paul VI expressed the Christocentric attitude of the Council and its vision of the Church with surprising clarity. "Christ,"

---

3. Constitution on the Church, No. 5.

he said, "is our starting point, Christ is our way and our leader, Christ our hope and our final goal. . . . No other light than Christ shall shine on our assembly. . . . We will say with the liturgy: We know only you, Christ."—"Christ is the light of all nations. . . . By her relationship with Christ, the Church is a kind of sacrament or sign of intimate union with God, and of the unity of all mankind. She is also an instrument for the achievement of such union and unity. . . . The conditions of this age lend special urgency to the Church's task of bringing all men to full union with Christ, since mankind today is joined together more closely than ever before by social, technical, and cultural bonds."[4]

This Christocentric view must be applied to moral theology. For a consciously Christocentric view of the Church is impossible unless it is applied to the Church's life, to the celebration of the liturgy, doctrinal teaching and its legal and administrative structures. Such a connection and mutual dependence are particularly evident in the relation between our understanding of the Church and moral theology. We need not be prophets in order to forecast that the deeper Christocentric ecclesiology of Vatican II will also have its effects on scientific moral theology and moral preaching. If this were not to happen, the ecclesiology of the Council would have no permanent influence.

What, then, is our view of the fundamental structure of a Christocentric moral theology which at the same time manifests the true nature of the Church?

Christ is the law, that is to say the most intimate law of the life of the Church as well as of the individual Christian.

Basing themselves on the Scriptures, the earliest theologians

---

4. AAS 45 (1963) 846; **Constitution on the Church**, No. 1.

of the Church call Christ "the law and the covenant." This is certainly central to the theology of Justin the Martyr: "We do not place our hope in Moses nor in the Law. Matters are quite different: for I have read that there will be a final law and a covenant firmer than all, which God now commands all to preserve if they want a share in God's inheritance.... Christ has been given us as the eternal and final law and as the faithful covenant, apart from whom there is neither law nor instruction nor commandment.... From his works and the miracles which accompany them all can realize that he is the new law and the new covenant."[5] The law of Moses and circumcision give way to "the blood of the Redeemer, in which we believe. Now another covenant and another law have gone forth from Sion, Jesus Christ.... Therefore let us walk in the light of the Lord."[6] Christ, the Son of God, who was born from a virgin according to the will of the Father, from the progeny of Abraham, from the tribe of Judah, from the house of David, was announced to the world beforehand as the eternal law, the new covenant."[7] Like Justin, Irenaeus, too, explicitly applies the words of Scripture "He appointed a law in Israel" (Ps. 77 (78):5) to the Person of Christ;[8] sim-

---

5. **Dialogue with Trypho** 11, PG 6, 497ff. Justin the Martyr (c. 100-c. 165) was a philosopher and convert from paganism and a so-called "apologist" of Christianity. His two most famous works are his **First Apology**, a defence of Christianity against paganism, and the **Dialogue with Trypho**, a reply to Judaism. Trans.

6. **Dialogue with Trypho** 24, PG 6, 528. The punctuation in the manuscripts is not always consistent. But in any case, there can be no doubt that in this passage, too, Justin regards Christ himself as the covenant of the Law.

7. **Ibid.** 43, PG 6, 568; also 51, 599; 65, 122, 625; 122, 760.

8. **Adversus haereses** 1, III c. 16, 3; PG 7, 923. Irenaeus (c. 130-c. 200) was the greatest early theologian of the Eastern Church; **Adversus**

ilarly also the words of the prophet Isaiah (2:3): "For out of Zion shall go forth the law, and the word of the Lord from Jerusalem."[9] Clement of Alexandria says this in almost the same words: "The law of the Lord is blameless. It leads the souls home. The Savior himself is called law and word; thus in the kerygma of Peter and already in Isaiah: 'For out of Zion shall go forth the law, and the word of the Lord from Jerusalem.' "[10] In the *Stromateis* Clement speaks of the image of God in the soul of the true "gnostic," in whom Christ reigns through man's obedience to faith, Christ, "who is truly the law, the commandment and the eternal word."[11] A similar passage occurs in the *Shepherd of Hermas*: "This great tree which overshadows plains and mountains and all the earth is the law of God which was given to the whole world; and this law is the Son of God preached unto the ends of the earth."[12]

---

haereses (Against the Heresies) is his principal work, directed chiefly against the heresy of Gnosticism. Trans.

9. Adversus haereses 1, IV, c. 34, 4; PG 7, 1085f.

10. Eclogae 57, PG 9, 728. Clement of Alexandria (c. 150-c. 215), was a philosopher-theologian and teacher at the Catechetical School of Alexandria, which represented one of the mainstreams of Christian thought in the ancient Eastern Church. His principal work is the Stromateis (Miscellaneous Studies), others are the Protrepticus or "Exhortation to the Greeks" and the Paedagogue, a treatise on Christian life. The Eclogae are excerpts from other writings and notes to be used for his own works; it would seem that the passage quoted by the author goes back to Irenaeus. Trans.

11. Stromateis 1, VII, c. 3; PG 9, 421. Clement's "gnostic" means the perfect Christian, especially the contemplative; he is not to be confused with someone subscribing to the gnostic heresy. Trans.

12. Pastor Hermae, Similitude VIII, 3, 2. I have used the translation of J. B. Lightfoot. The Shepherd of Hermas is a second century work of

These few quotations from famous early Fathers show that in those days the moral message of Christianity was presented wholly in Christocentric and personal terms, perfectly faithful to the teaching of Christ himself, who is at the center of it as the source of life, the way of salvation and the life-giving truth. This message was faithful to St. Paul who summed up everything in the "law of Christ" (Gal 6:2), which is basically none other than the love of Christ indwelling and urging us, so that we live "in Christ" as in our law (*ennomos Christou*, 1 Cor 9:21). We are the property of Christ, trusting in his name, his power and his grace, impelled and guided by his Spirit, finding thus the truly liberating law of Christian existence.

John XXIII followed exactly this line in the text which he wanted inscribed over the doors of the Council: "If Christ grows in us because we are lovingly putting into practice the truths he taught, we shall be on the road to true progress." But this growth of Christ in us is always indissolubly united to the Church's growth in love and to its being filled with the love of Christ "the fullness of him who fills all in all" (Eph 1:23; cf. 4:13).

Christ is the covenant. The law of the Old Testament was promulgated as the "law of the covenant," and so the New Testament law, too, must be seen under the aspect of a new covenant. And this is principally realized in Christ himself, spreading to all men through the working of the Holy Spirit. In a unique way Christ himself is the New Covenant, both ontologically and existentially. Divinity and humanity meet in the hypostatic union of the incarnate Word, we might also say in the "hypostatic covenant," which is the most intimate,

---

an otherwise unknown author treating of a series of visions. Trans.

vigorous and indissoluble form of covenant. "All these things, however, were done by way of preparation and as a figure of that new and perfect covenant which was to be ratified in Christ, and of that more luminous revelation which was to be given through God's very Word made flesh ... Christ instituted this new covenant, that is to say the new testament, in his blood (cf. 1 Cor 11:25), by calling together a people made up of Jew and Gentile, making them one, not according to the flesh but in the Spirit. This was to be the new People of God.... The heritage of this people are the dignity and freedom of the sons of God, in whose hearts the Holy Spirit dwells as in his temple. Its law is the new commandment to love as Christ loved us (cf. Jn 13:34)."[13]

The same truth may be expressed in the basic biblical categories of "word and response," which are to be understood as centered in God and Christ, but at the same time in a personal and saving social (*heilssozial*) sense.

Christ is the final and perfect covenant, for he is the Word in which the Father expresses himself fully from all eternity, by whom he communicates his love and his saving plan to us men through the mysteries of the incarnation, the passion and death, the resurrection and ascension of his only begotten Son. Christ himself and all he does, says and gives, commands and suffers, is the Word God addresses to us, not a transient and ineffective word, but the Word that remains eternally. The center of the Christian moral law becomes visible only in him. Without him, all is dead and dumb, at most a sounding word, which, if it is taken seriously at all, finally forces a man to ask who is speaking this word. This is true also of the natural moral law. It exists only because all subsists through

---

13. **Constitution on the Church**, No. 9.

the Word: "Without him was not anything made that was made" (Jn 1:3). The ultimate finality of all created things, including the natural moral law, is expressed only in Christ Jesus, the Word made man. "For in him all things were created . . . all things were created through him and for him. . . . He is the head of the body, the Church" (Col 1:16).

Christ alone gives creation the power to make a final answer. He himself is the answer in the name of redeemed humanity. "In him all things hold together" (Col 1:17), also insofar as everything is summed up in him for the final answer of love and adoration before the heavenly Father.

The morning and evening prayer of his life bears witness that Christ understood himself and his whole life to be an answer. His human nature and its hypostatic union was for him a gift of the Father, and the goal of his life was: "Lo, I have come to do thy will" (Heb 10:7). His answer is a perfect sacrifice: "Into thy hands I commit my spirit" (Lk 23:46). He answers in the name of all mankind. Thus the goal of salvation history and of the Christian life is that man should know himself to be called by Christ in his whole existence and should answer with all he is and has. This is no arbitrary or independent decision of man. It is the inner dynamic of his existence created in the Word of God and renewed in Christ. Man can understand himself, his nature, destiny and highest possibilities only insofar as he both listens to Christ and answers with him.

This listening and responding attitude frees man from his deadly self-glorification and redeems him to true responsibility. Man finds his true self only in union with Christ.

The Church is the true "qahal." It is the *ekklesia* that has been called from "not-being the-people-of-God." As the body of Christ it is the gathering call (*ekklesia* and *kalein* have the same root: to call). The Church lives in Christ, who is the Word of God to mankind and to all creation, and it may transmit his word to all. But it can credibly do so only if it lives and is united by his call and in the answer of his love. "At all times and among every people, God has given welcome to whosoever fears him and does what is right (cf. Acts 10:35). It has pleased God, however, to make men holy and save them not merely as individuals without any mutual bonds, but by making them into a single people which acknowledges in truth and serves him in holiness."[14]

It is easy to see that Catholic morality is dialogical, personal, and related to the community, and precisely as Christocentric and ecclesial morality it is concerned with social salvation (*heilssozial*). Only thus can it teach Christians to express the mystery of Christ and the true nature of the Church in their lives and to reveal them to others.

It is important to see that the various aspects and characteristics of the Christian life are not isolated but have one center in Christ, through whom they are organically one: "So it is that this messianic people, although it does not actually include all men, and may more than once look like a small flock, is nonetheless a lasting and sure seed of unity, hope, and salvation for the whole human race. Established by Christ as a fellowship of life, charity and truth, it is also used by him as an instrument for the redemption of all and is sent forth into the whole world as the light of the world and the salt of the earth (cf. Mt 5:13-16)."[15]

It is one of the most important truths of the mystery of the Church that its relation to Christ is not merely external.

---

14. Constitution on the Church, No. 9.
15. Constitution on the Church, No. 9.

The Church is the body of Christ, Christ lives in it and enlivens it through this Holy Spirit. Thus it is also in the life of every believer: as long as a Christian regards his relation to Christ as something external, rendering him only outward obedience, he has not yet grasped the true meaning of the New Law. For the mystery of the Christian life is the truth that Christ lives in us and that we are in him, as St. Paul has affirmed more than one hundred sixty times in his Letters. Christian life is a communion of life in Christ, expressed above all in the solidarity of salvation (*Heilssolidaritate*) of all members of the Church and in their zeal for all men. Christ the Lord, High Priest taken from among men (cf. Heb 5:1-5), made a kingdom and priests to God his Father (Apoc 1:6; cf. 5:9-10) out of this new people. The baptized, by regeneration and the anointing of the Holy Spirit, are consecrated into a spiritual house and a holy priesthood. Thus through all those works befitting Christian men they can offer spiritual sacrifices and proclaim the power of him who has called them out of darkness into his marvellous light (cf. 1 Pet 2:4-10).... Everywhere on earth they must bear witness to Christ and give an answer to those who seek an account of that hope of eternal life which is in them (cf. 1 Pet 3:15).[16]

Several important aspects of Catholic morality result from this view:

If a man fails to respond to some special graces or to a particular need of his neighbor whom he might help with his natural or supernatural gifts, claiming that the general written law does not demand this, he not only deprives himself of some special merit, but says "No" to Christ, who wants his Body to grow through him. If such an attitude becomes a

---

16. **Constitution on the Church,** No. 10.

principle, he rejects the law of life in Christ Jesus, hiding behind a merely legalistic attitude.

If a man does not live in accordance with grace or consciously delays his conversion to such a life, he does not live according to the Christian law, even if his actions accord with the external law. Nothing avails us if the love of Christ is not living and active in us. This indwelling of Christ reveals itself above all in our gradual liberation from anthropocentrism, from a narrow concern with our own perfection and in our increasing commitment to the "new commandment" of love for our neighbor.

Love is no mere commandment added to the finished constitution of the Church. The Church itself is the "mystery of love." It receives its life from the open wound in the heart of Jesus. As the bride of Christ, freely chosen by grace, the Church lives by the love that creates it. Its principle of life is the Holy Spirit whom Christ, as its Redeemer, sends it as a sign and earnest of his infinite love. Through the Holy Spirit the Church is integrated into the love of Christ which gives itself back to the Father and sacrifices itself for men. Thus, by living according to its true nature, the Church can announce the mystery of Christ to the world. In all it is, has and does, the Church, which itself is love, is called to make the love of Christ visible, as Christ has taught us to experience that God is love. "The holy People of God shares also in Christ's prophetic office. It spreads abroad a living witness to him, especially by means of a life of faith and charity and by offering to God a sacrifice of praise, the tribute of lips which give honor to his name (cf. Heb 13:15)."[17]

Hence the commandment of love is not added as some-

---

17. Constitution on the Church, No. 12.

thing external to the juridical structures of the Church. It is exactly the reverse. Christ has found a visible Church with a certain constitution, offices and services, in order to show that she is his beloved bride who is to unite all men in the answer of love. In the course of history the Church will add to its essential constitution or live it in a certain way, but all this is subject to, and judged by its inmost mission, which is love. Privileges, external forms, customs, laws, administrative institutions and whatever else in human tradition is ultimately of value only insofar as it serves to announce the love of God in the form of witness and of life. Even in the first session of Vatican II, presided over by John XXIII, everything was examined according to this principle. Whatever does not help, but rather prevents the message of the primacy of love from being credibly announced to the men of our time and to all cultures and social classes, all this must either be changed or sacrificed according to this principle, while new things must be started and carefully fostered in the same way.

The Church of the incarnate Word knows that juridical structures, administrative institutions, money and many other visible and perishable things are needed during its pilgrimage. But these must never become independent. They always justify their existence anew by proving that they serve the saving message of the love of God and neighbor.

This means that there must be the appropriate emphases. The body is meant to mirror the spirit. But if the former is stressed too much, to a certain degree it hides and suppresses the spirit. The earthly aspects of the Church such as law and administration may predominate so much that they fail to express the spirit of love and may even someway betray it.

Anyone who knows the history of moral theology will see at once the relations between this and the concept of the

Church. The ecclesiology of Vatican II undoubtedly corresponds to Scripture and the most vital tradition and must also be reflected in the moral instruction of priests so that it may be continued in preaching and inform the whole ecclesial life.

Not only the treatise on the Church, but the whole moral theology must be a synthesis, at the center of which is Christ with his personal gift and demand of love. It does not suffice to teach in passing in one treatise, beside or even after the others, that the love of God and neighbor is "the fulfilling of the law" (Rom 13:10). It must emerge from every paragraph that what matters is love, and that all the virtues of the Christian are but means and expressions of the love of God and neighbor. A moral theology which is meant to be scientific and to form good pastors and good Christians must be characterized by the primacy of love after the example of the writings of John, the beloved disciple, and the apostle of the Gentiles. "All of Christ's faithful, therefore, whatever be the conditions, duties, and circumstances of their lives, will grow in holiness day by day through these very situations, if they accept all of them with faith from the hand of their heavenly Father, and if they cooperate with the divine will by showing every man through their earthly activities the love with which God has loved the world."[18]

It is quite impossible first to present the Christian life as lived under the Ten Commandments given on Sinai, and then also to add the commandment of loving God and one's neighbor. This would even be quite inferior to the Old Covenant.

It is impossible to treat love of one's neighbor as a subsection of the fifth commandment, as is still done in some

---

18. **Constitution on the Church,** No. 41.

catechisms. If one wants to follow the schema of the ten commandments, these must be interpreted as expressions of the love of God and neighbor.

It is equally impossible to treat of the sacraments as of a new cycle of duties after the commandments. They are gifts and deeds of the love of Christ, powerful signs of salvation from which grow the dignity, grace and demands of the Christian life. It must become clear from the place of the sacraments in the system of morality that the primacy of love does not involve three "sets of duties," but the presence of the love of God in Jesus Christ and in the Church through the Holy Spirit. Love is not primarily a duty, but a gift which makes the most urgent claims.

If man's intellectual powers are completely occupied with legal casuistry not illuminated by love, it does not help much to admit either before or afterwards that love has the primacy and must inform the whole Christian life. This approach to morality produced many scrupulous Catholics who were exclusively occupied with legal niceties, rubrics and taboos to such an extent that they could no longer hear the message of God's love; for them this shift of emphasis in moral questions obscured the true nature of the Church.

The Church of the Second Vatican Council considers it necessary to simplify canon law and to emphasize more clearly the primacy of love; this attitude will certainly not diminish reverence for the law and the will to obey. But all this can influence the Christian life only if moral teaching and preaching clearly follow the direction initiated by the Council. It can hardly be denied by one conversant with the subject that much remains to be done in this matter.

In his last greeting to the community — the "Church"— at Corinth, St. Paul mentions, together with Christ and the primacy of love, the fellowship of the Holy Spirit: "The grace of the Lord Jesus Christ and the love of God and the fellowship of the Holy Spirit be with you all" (2 Cor 13:14). The Church can bear witness to the mystery of Christ in its life only through a living faith in the Holy Spirit and in obedience to him; and only thus can it convince men that the incarnate Son of God has given it the same love and power with which he himself had been sent by the Father.

Vatican II's image of the Church is characterized by the words of Pius XII: "If Christ is the head of the Church, the Holy Spirit is its soul."[19] The Holy Spirit does not dwell in the Church as in a living home; he also effects its building up into the fullness of the Body of Christ. The faithful are a holy community in Christ Jesus only through his grace: "You are no longer strangers and sojourners, but you are fellow citizens with the saints and members of the household of God, built upon the foundation of the apostles and prophets, Christ Jesus himself being the cornerstone in whom the whole structure is joined together and grows into a holy temple in the Lord; in whom you also are built into it for a dwelling place of God in the Spirit" (Eph 2:19-22). "The Spirit dwells in the Church and in the hearts of the faithful as in a temple (cf. 1 Cor 3:16; 6:19). In them he prays and bears witness to the fact that they are adopted sons (cf. Gal 4:6; Rom 8:15-16 and 26). The Spirit guides the Church into the fullness of truth (cf. Jn 16:13) and gives her a unity of fellowship and service. He furnishes and directs her with various gifts, both hierarchical and charismatic, and adorns her with the fruits of his grace (cf. Eph 4:11-12; 1 Cor 12:4; Gal 5:22)."[20]

19. Encyclical "Mystici Corporis"; AAS 10 (1943) 220.
20. Constitution on the Church, No. 4.

The ecclesiology of Vatican II will make it impossible to regard the Church first and foremost as an external organization divided into commanding officers and subjects. Certainly, authority and obedience must be honored in the Church of Christ, but in a more sublime, spiritual way. The ministry and offices of the Church must be viewed from a theological standpoint, that is to say from the workings of the Spirit of Christ as expressed in Eph 4 and 1 Cor 12. All ministries, ranks and functions serve the building up of the body of Christ in mysterious unity. But unity in love is ultimately the grace of the Holy Spirit: "All these are inspired by one and the same Spirit, who apportions to each one individually as he wills" (1 Cor 12:11): "For by one Spirit we were all baptized into one body" (*ibid.* v. 13): this faith moves every Christian most urgently to realize his own vocation in unity, faithfulness and service to the mystical Body: "One body and one Spirit, just as you were called to the one hope that belongs to your call" (Eph 4:4).

The modern world, and especially the totalitarian regimes, trusts in strict organization wanting to make everything uniform and to level everything, whereas the Church believes in the one Spirit who unites in multiplicity and diversity. In this way we must understand the collegiality of the bishops under the successor of Peter, the variety of the renewed liturgy, the struggle for more unified and yet more varied pastoral work and the apostolate of the laity. Believing and trusting in the Holy Spirit, who is the bond of unity and peace, the Church conquers the fearful temptation to expect unity only or at least mainly from the juridical bond, and thus to succumb to an unwholesome uniformity and Latinization, and to a centralization that is incompatible with the principle of subsidiarity. The greater the joy of faith and the happier the obedience to the Holy Spirit, the more harmoniously can the Church combine unity with diversity and diversity with unity. Not to risk this would betray a fatally weak faith in the mystery of the Holy Spirit to which the whole structure of the Church must bear witness.

"Thus in their diversity all bear witness to the admirable unity of the Body of Christ. This very diversity of graces, ministries, and works gathers the children of God into one, because 'all these things are the work of one and the same Spirit'" (1 Cor 12:11).[21]

The presentation of the moral message in theology as well as in catechizing and preaching, hence also in the Christian life, must show forth this "communion of the Holy Spirit." It must become evident that the law of Christ is a law of freedom and at the same time of the highest solidarity, that the ecclesiastical laws are animated by the spiritual law of life in Christ Jesus and need spiritual understanding and fulfillment; that the love and communion of the Holy Spirit must show themselves in the ordering of the individual gifts of God towards the spiritual building-up of the community. Thus we are provided with essential signs for the discernment of spirits.

The apostle of the Gentiles speaks in the same breath of the "law of the Spirit" which sets us free from the law of sin (Rom 8:2) and of the "liberty of the children of God" (Rom 8:21). The link between the two is an absolute, childlike obedience to the Holy Spirit: "For all who are led by the Spirit of God are sons of God" (Rom 8:13).

Catholic moral theologians ought not try to whittle down the tension, or, better, the "contrast-harmony" between solidarity and initiative by overemphasizing either the one or the

---

21. **Constitution on the Church,** No. 32.

other. The virtue of *epikeia* must be given back its traditional place with regard to obeying positive laws. This, however, can safely be done only if the concept of *epikeia* is freed from the fetters of individualistic and comfortably selfish thought. *Epikeia* is a virtue of lawgivers and authorities, who may not demand anything unjust and must not quench the spirit of spontaneity and initiative. This virtue is uniquely necessary for ecclesiastical lawgivers and authorities; for if they were devoid of it they would betray the essence of their witness to the Church as a community of confirmed, courageous Christians led by the Holy Spirit. But the subject, too, is not a spiritual man if he is guided by laziness and egoism and sticks to the letter of the law or falsely claims to act in accordance with *epikeia*.

The religious individualism of the past century was compensated by legal inflexibility to such an extent that sometimes merely positive laws took absolute precedence over the demands of God written in the hearts of men and over the demands of the present moment. This development had an inner logic; for a man who thinks individualistically even in the ultimate questions of salvation cannot be expected to make a proper use of freedom, especially not of *epikeia*. Unless the spirit of Christian freedom and responsibility is to be suffocated by legalistic pettiness and mistrust, the whole Christian life must be founded on "the law of the spirit of life in Christ Jesus." This involves courageous freedom as well as a total lack of selfishness; it is true freedom in "the communion of the Holy Spirit."

The soul of ecclesiastical legislation and of obedience to it is not to be sought in a metaphysical foundation of individual ecclesiastical laws; on the contrary, the difference between positive laws and the eternally valid demands of metaphysics must be made more evident. The positive laws of the Church are truly "spiritual," that is inspired by the Spirit and according to the "law of the spirit," insofar as they express openness to the "signs of the times." It goes without saying that they must not contradict the nature of man; but this is not enough: they must above all be faithful to the working of God in salvation history, they must respond to the historical opportunities.

In a time of tremendous historical changes the Church must boldly adapt its legislation; but if it is not to act recklessly and imprudently, it must also use the human means offered to it by divine providence in order to understand the signs of the times. The Church is not only the community of the Holy Spirit, so that it is capable in principle of spiritually understanding the time in humility and love; it is also the Church of the incarnate Word; hence it must make use of every suitable human means for the salvation of souls. Moral theologians who emphasize once more the law of the spirit will not succumb to an unhealthy spiritualism if they use psychology and sociology boldly but with caution.

After the middle of the nineteenth century in Germany, too, the moral theology of Johann Michael Sailer, Johann Baptist Hirscher and Magnus Jocham was supplanted by the stereotyped moral handbooks which at first sight undoubtedly seemed more in line with ecclesiastical tradition than the works of these three great exponents of a spiritualized moral doctrine. Today, however, we are beginning to realize that the ecclesiality of the canonistic type of moral handbooks was too external and too narrow, for it was almost exclusively concentrated on the category of legal obedience.

A new and deeper ecclesiology which had made a vigorous start with the encyclical *Mystici Corporis* and reached a high-water mark at the Second Vatican Council goes back to Sailer, Hirscher and Jocham, but goes far beyond them: Christian morality is thoroughly ecclesial and related to the Church, the mystery of salvation.

Because today we have to defend ourselves against collectivism, we have developed sensitivity for the uniqueness of every human being, we have become open for the "existential." This spirit of our times could easily degenerate into individualism, but need not do so. This is prevented by the knowledge that everyone must discover and use his own particular possibilities precisely for the sake of those treasures we have in common. The ecclesial sense must be expressed not only in obedience to general laws, but also in everything belonging to individual or existential ethics, for all gifts are bestowed by the Holy Spirit, so that everyone should contribute to building up the mystical body with all he is and has.

One of the most important problems of moral theology and moral pedagogics is the profound organic connection between the categories of community and individual. The same question appears when we are trying to produce a synthesis between the community apostolate and the spontaneous "Yes" of the individual to the chances Providence offers him in the service of God. The true synthesis results from the right view of the Christian life as "community in the Holy Spirit."

Though the ecclesiology of the Second Vatican Council is decidedly spiritual (*pneumatisch*), it nevertheless does not tend towards a spiritualism which sees salvation only in terms of the invisible soul or adds it as a separate item. Beginning with Pope John's opening speech, all the documents of Vatican II, in accordance with the mind of modern man, stress the Church of the Word Incarnate. This Church listens to the spirit of the time in order to strengthen and purify all the powers of life it contains. Even Pius XI and Pius XII had clearly recognized the duty of the Church to preach the mystery of the Incarnation not only as a saving event of the past, but also as a present happening of salvation which gives its norms to the action of the Church, and which must be expressed not only in doctrinal formulas, but by integrating the modern world, into all cultures and social structures. Surely the teaching and the pastoral and legal reforms of the Second Vatican Council consistently express this truth: "The Church, or, in other words, the kingdom of Christ now present in mystery, grows visibly in the world through the power of God. . . . All men are called to this union with Christ, who is the light of the world, from whom we go forth, through whom we live, and toward whom our journey leads us."[22]

It may, of course, be said that moral theologians have always taken reality seriously: they have always taught the virtue of prudence, which deals with the matter of reality, and they have always been concerned with integrating what is truly good in real life. The question, however, is this, whether they have palpably and visibly shown that all this is concerned with the fundamental saving mystery of the Incarnation.

In a superficially "baptized" philosophical ethic prudence is chiefly regarded with a view to the self-perfection of the individual. It seems to be based mainly on human planning. A doctrine of the Christian virtue of prudence based on the

---

22. **Constitution on the Church,** No. 3. This truth is expressed as a principle for the first time in the **Pastoral Constitution on the Church in the Modern World.** The **Decree on the Church's Missionary Activity** (Dec. 7, 1965), is imbued with the same spirit.

saving mystery of the Church is not only theocentric, but is also concerned with the history and the social aspects of salvation. The judgment of prudence must take account of the present moment (*kairós*), which God, the Lord of salvation history, has prepared in order to integrate the forces of the new aeon into the stuff of history. Here again the category of the "existential" must be seen in the context of the continuity of historical action. It thus becomes clear that existential ethics is not arbitrary and abrupt discontinuity, but means grasping the often modest, though unique chances of the historical moment in faithful obedience to salvation history as a whole.

The presence of the Church in medieval and modern politics has not had good results. Today the Church wants to be present in every department of life like a leaven, like the salt that shows its strength when it is dissolved or the light which radiates in consuming itself. In all its activities in the world the Church must imitate the incarnation of the Word of God who "emptied himself" (Phil 2:7). In the Christian milieu the splendor of the paschal mystery does not even begin to shine forth if the activities of Christians do not bear witness to the mystery of the incarnation. "Christ, having been lifted up from the earth, is drawing all men to himself (Jn 12:32, Greek text). Rising from the dead (cf. Rom 6:9), he sent his life-giving Spirit upon his disciples and through this Spirit has established his body, the Church, as the universal sacrament of salvation. . . . The final age of the world has already come upon us (cf. 1 Cor 10:11). The renovation of the world has been irrevocably decreed and in this age is already anticipated in some real way."[23]

---

23. **Constitution on the Church**, No. 48.

Today's moral theologians must continue the promising start of a "theology of earthly things"[24] which the Second Vatican Council has outlined especially in the *Pastoral Constitution on the Church in the Modern World* and, while doing so, they must emphasize the mystery of the Incarnation more than, for example, the exponents of the *Devotio Moderna* and their spiritual descendants.

The "natural moral law" comprises all the moral norms necessarily involved in the fact of being human which are accessible to human reason, at least in principle. Since today Catholics are prepared to collaborate widely with all men of good will, the natural law has become much more important, because it forms a bridge between them. On the other hand, if in this undertaking Christians are not to lose the sense of what is their own special inheritance, moral theologians must also show more clearly how the natural moral law is integrated in the law of Christ. For there must not be even the slightest semblance of a discrepancy. The natural law, too, must be considered from an essentially Christological point of view: "All things were created through him and for him. He is before all things, and in him all things hold together" (Col 1:16f). The pagans who find the natural law in their heart and live accordingly, they, too, live by the light and strength of Christ as "anonymous Christians."

Some people, including certain Catholic theologians, still have the incredible idea that the moral teaching of the New Testament adds no new content to the natural law, that it only offers new motives. This is actually worse than the moral doctrine of Pelagius, who also asserted it, though only

24. Cf. G. Thils, **Theologie der irdischen Wirklichkeiten,** Salzburg, 1955; **Théologie et réalité sociale,** Tournai, 1952.

verbally, for he presupposed a different concept of nature, namely the historically given nature which was ordered towards Christ from the beginning. Thus Pelagius obscured "only" the uniqueness of the New Covenant, but not the fact that all Christian morality is centered in Christ. If the newness of Christian morality is merely added to the doctrine of natural law as a motivation, without a content of its own, then the merely natural dominates completely: the "supernatural" of such a morality is lacking in, and estranged from, being; it is merely an adjunct to natural being and the natural foundation of Christian morality.

This position is explained by the legal concept of morality, according to which morality is only concerned with defining frontiers and is based on imposed formulas instead of on being. The decisive starting point of New Testament morality is the "being in Christ"; as opposed to a conceivable pure nature, this means a tremendous new fullness of being which nevertheless embraces the whole man, who through grace is in Christ Jesus. Another trait of Christian morality corresponds to this essentially ontological and personal view: It is not a kind of "frontier morality," but is seen decisively from the point of view of its ideal goal which has received a new fullness from being in Christ. Both the norm and the motive are truly new in the new commandment: "As I have loved you" (Jn 15:12).

The eschatological Church can say to the world in the joy of salvation: "The time is fulfilled, and the kingdom of God is at hand" (Mk 1:15). It lives from the grace which it has already received and which teaches it to use the present time, but it must always bear witness to the fact that it is completely directed towards "the blessed hope, the appearing of the glory of our great God and Savior Jesus Christ" (Tit 2:13).

Detached from all transitory forms and from all desire for earthly prestige, it must testify that "the form of this world is passing away" (1 Cor 7:31). Patiently working and always trying to make all spheres of life more Christian, the Church professes its faith in the kingdom of God which is already present, but also its hope in the "new heaven and the new earth" which are completely and visibly realized only with the Second Coming of the Lord.

The eschatological Church is always already united to the Church of the heavenly Jerusalem, in whose songs of praise it joins even now. But precisely this must warn it against any kind of "triumphalism," for it sings these hymns as a pilgrim, as the Church of the mean-time, of the time of penance: "Just as Christ carried out the work of redemption in poverty and oppression, so the Church is called to follow the same path in communicating to men the fruits of salvation. Christ Jesus, 'though he was by nature God . . . emptied himself, taking the nature of a slave' (Phil 2:6); and 'being rich, he became poor' (2 Cor 8:9) for our sakes. Thus, although the Church needs human resources to carry out her mission, she is not set up to seek earthly glory, but to proclaim humility and self-sacrifice, even by her own example."[25] Just these aspects of the Church's image are of the greatest importance for our dialogue with our separated Christian brethren.

Thus the whole Christian life must express and bear witness to this eschatological character of the Church and the mystery of Christ. These are the true conditions for effectively overcoming the view of Christianity as a bourgeois institution, materialism and the discontinuity of a false existentialism.

The Christian life is lived in the fruitful tension between

---

25. **Constitution on the Church**, No. 8.

what is already present and what is not yet fulfilled. The Christian is never satisfied with himself precisely because of what he has received as a "new creation." What we call triumphalism is related to Pharisaism, the attitude that does not look towards what lies before us nor on what is given us by God, for smug self-satisfaction is impossible in either case.

Christian life and Christian striving must be bold and humble at the same time. They are a glad and grateful affirmation of the law of Christ, else they are not truly Christian. On the other hand, they are also judged by Christ, but this judgment does not oppress the man who humbles himself while also pressing forward.

The commandment: "You, therefore, must be perfect, as your heavenly Father is perfect" (Mt 5:48) corresponds to the sanctification we have already received and to the goal that is before us, that is of following Christ with an undivided mind. Since the love of God has already been generously poured forth into our hearts by the Holy Spirit, we can even now at least begin to do the will of God on earth as it is done in heaven, according to the measure of love we have received. But we must still implore God to help us.

While the commandment of the perfect love of God and our neighbor expresses the eschatological fullness of salvation, the necessity of detailed, limiting commandments expresses the "not yet" of the time between beginning and fulfillment.

A deeper understanding of the eschatological Church must produce the right balance between these two kinds of commandments.

The *Constitution on the Liturgy* as well as the other documents of Vatican II which deal with the mystery of the Church are unmistakably centered in the mystery of Christ's priesthood, by which the Church lives and through which it is completely ordered to the glory of God without any false self-glorification. The mystery of redemption is enacted in the mysteries of faith, in the Eucharist and all the sacraments, but also in the life of the faithful, who are thus redeemed from their man-centered existence and live for the glory of God. The Church is the family of God, the community of salvation, worship and faith, and through this faith and their common hope and love in Christ Jesus men must bring back all things to the glory of God: "For this God finally sent his Son's Spirit as Lord and Lifegiver. He it is who, on behalf of the whole Church and each and every one of those who believe, is the principle of their coming together and remaining together in the teaching of the apostles and in fellowship, in the breaking of bread and in prayers (cf. Acts 2:42; Greek text).... For all the faithful scattered throughout the world are in communion with each other in the Holy Spirit, so that "he who occupies the See of Rome knows the people of India are his members" (John Chrysostom).... This characteristic of universality which adorns the People of God is a gift from the Lord himself. By reason of it, the Catholic Church strives energetically and constantly to bring all humanity with all its riches back to Christ its Head in the unity of his Spirit."[26]

Our time is threatened by laicism and a non-religious conception of the world, hence moral theology and all the preaching of the Church must make it emphatically clear that the honor and glory of God is the highest goal. Men will once more learn to understand what sin is only if they recover the sense of worship and practice it more profoundly.

According to the *Constitution of the Sacred Liturgy*, this

---

26. Constitution on the Church, No. 13.

"liturgy is the outstanding means by which the faithful can express in their lives, and manifest to others, the mystery of Christ and the real nature of the true Church." If this is so, then the liturgy must also occupy a central place in moral theology. It is impossible to treat the sacraments and the Eucharistic sacrifice only after the commandments as a new cycle of requirements as an additional help in the fulfillment of duties conceived quite independently of the sacramental life. In the same way as the theological virtues the sacraments, too, must inform every treatise of moral theology.

In recent times the sacraments have occasionally been presented almost exclusively as "means of grace" or of healing. This was a very grave diminishment of the order of salvation. For the sacraments are a personal encounter with Christ in call and response, in giving and receiving a task." They express the indissoluble community of salvation in Christ Jesus and the Church. They are principally worship, in which God glorifies his saving justice and mercy, and in which Christ sanctifies men and integrates them into his high-priestly activity. Sacramental life is the saving action which is co-ordinated to the final act of history, when Christ surrenders all things to the Father "that God may be everything to every-one" (1 Cor 15:28).

"For as long as all of us, who are sons of God and comprise one family in Christ (cf. Heb 3:6), remain in communion with one another in mutual charity and in one praise of the most Holy Trinity, we are responding to the deepest vocation of the Church and partaking in a foretaste of the liturgy of consummate glory. For when Christ shall appear and the

---

27. For a more detailed discussion see my book, **Gabe und Auftrag der Sakramente**, Salzburg, 1962.

glorious resurrection of the dead takes place, the splendor of God will brighten the heavenly city and the Lamb will be the lamp thereof (cf. Apoc 21:24). Then in the supreme happiness of charity the whole Church of the saints will adore God and 'the Lamb who was slain' (Apoc 5:12), proclaiming with one voice: 'To him who sits upon the throne, and to the Lamb, blessing and honor and glory and dominion, for ever and ever'" (Apoc 5:13-14).[28]

---

28. Constitution on the Church, No. 51.

3

MORAL THEOLOGY AND THE APOSTOLIC FORMATION OF PRIESTS

In the last centuries, that is to say in the post-Tridentine period up to the Second Vatican Council, moral instruction in the seminaries has been almost exclusively a special training for future confessors. In the light of Vatican II, however, we may well hope that future moral theology will be far more clearly a training of the Christian and of the priest for a Christlike life. The priest must be trained, through moral theology, to become a courageous apostle rather than a mere controller of morals in the confessional, for only then can we hope that he will mediate a moral teaching which will form laymen, too, into apostles.

In No. 20 of the *Decree on Priestly Formation* of Vatican II it is said explicitly that priests "should be trained with exactness to ignite and fan the apostolic activity of laymen."[1]

The type of moral manuals like those by Noldin, Tanquerey and Aertnys-Damen originated in a closed society devoted to defense, not to call it in the climate of the ghetto. Post-Reformation Catholicism was anxious and shy. Neither priests nor faithful were prepared to take a constructive view of a frighteningly new world. The concern of moral theology was largely, even though not exclusively, to furnish the priest

---

1. Cf. also No. 16 of the same Decree, where Christian morality is said to have the aim "to bring forth fruit in charity for the life of the world," and the Decree on the Apostolate of the Laity, Nos. 25 and 30. Also The Decree on the Church's Missionary Activity, No. 39.

with simple, and often far too simplifying, principles and casuistic solutions which gave him a strict control of the consciences of the faithful and enabled him to distinguish accurately between mortal and venial sin and give precise instructions for their future activities. This kind of morality also reflects largely the absolutist climate of the age. It also had considerable positive aspects, for it fulfilled in a closed and protected society a function that should not be underestimated. However, it was never perfect, just as that age was one of the most difficult and also one of the most miserable periods of Church history. The much lamented legalism and juridicism can largely be explained by this one-sided view of moral theology. It should, however, not be forgotten that beside this moral teaching future priests were also instructed, even if only perfunctorily, in the subject of ascetic theology.

Today Catholics live in a pluralistic, open society. It no longer suffices to tell people in a village or a small town that obedience is the be-all and end-all of Christian attitudes. If the boys and girls of a village have only learned uncritical obedience in all things, they will also follow blindly any trends of their surroundings when they move to a big city. Today people can hold out against the influences of their surroundings only if they have learned to stand on their own feet. Faith must be enlightened, and consciences must be trained to assume responsibility. This is also more in accordance with the gospel than the "controlled morality" of the past two centuries.

A responsible morality means listening to the faith and surrendering one's whole life to God. It can exist only where there is faith in a personal God and his personal call. Christ himself is the Person of the Word and God's call, who was given us by the Father. In his divine Person Christ is the Word that comes from the Father and goes to the Father. In his incarnation he is the Word the Father addresses to us. In his redemption, in the paschal mystery he is the answer of redeemed humanity which the Father has accepted. To be integrated into Christ means being able to listen to the loving call of the heavenly Father, and to answer as a child and a friend of God.

Hence a morality of responsibility in the typically Christian sense means a most intimate unity of life and action with Christ. It means to be wholly given to the heavenly Father and to the longing of mankind for redemption.

The moral teaching of the last centuries should not be condemned *in toto*. It cannot, however, be denied that it promoted a strange mixture of individualism and mechanical legalism, even if this was not explicitly taught. A concern with individual salvation often caused a man to ask, like Luther: "How can I find a gracious God for myself," or, in the terms of moral textbooks and also of popular missionaries: "How do I save my soul?" which almost sounded like: "Save yourself if you can and leave the world to the evil one." Such an individualistic view of salvation was dangerous for the community. Hence it was compensated, and over-compensated, by a law imposed from outside which was often applied far too mechanically. In its best representatives, casuistry was a training for prudent judgments, but it became largely a recipe for mechanical application and easy control in the confessional, especially in the case of a none-too-wise confessor. This description, I admit, is exaggerated in parts. But I want to unmask a wrong tendency. For this mixture of legalism and individualism with regard to salvation was not free from anthropocentric and Pelagian touches, placing man and his concerns in the center of religion.

The biblical renewal of moral theology, on the other hand,

emphasized that all Christian thought and action must be formed by God and his kingdom and by his reign of love. Biblical morality is a morality of grace. While a morality which is only concerned with control in the confessional stresses uniformity, the morality of grace emphasizes the manifold gifts of grace, which are all given for the building up of the mystical body. An exaggerated morality of control suffocates the variety of graces and suppresses spontaneity. The morality of grace means both a humble listening and a courageous spontaneity, it takes risks and initiatives. A legal morality is imposed from outside and demands only a controllable minimum. A morality of grace, on the other hand, involves growth. Grace is a call to sanctity by which the Christian is asked to walk in the way of holiness, and holiness means to be wholly available for serving the glory of God and the salvation of men.

Simplifying, we may also say that the legalistic type of moral theology of the last two centuries was due to fear and suspicion, and that therefore the main emphasis was placed on legal uniformity. Thus spontaneity was suffocated. Men were scrupulously anxious to keep even the most minute laws. Moral theologians inculcated innumerable positive laws (according to Noldin, Prümmer and other authors about two hundred laws on the administration of the sacraments) under pain of eternal punishment (mortal sin — hell). Thus the attention of many priests and laymen was completely absorbed by rubrics and minor laws. Without being personally guilty, therefore, many priests resembled the Jewish priest in the gospel who passed by the man who had fallen among the robbers. Why did he pass him by? Because he had to observe his rubrics and his hair-splitting casuistics. For this reason he had no time left to follow the call of the moment.

Against this, biblical morality and the present renewal of moral theology emphasize especially the fundamental attitude of observing the will of God as it is expressed in the need of the hour. Our Lord himself emphasized again and again that he was waiting for his hour, or that his hour had come. He asks Christians to watch, because they do not know when the Lord will come. This does not only apply to his final coming, but to every hour in which a man is called, which prepares the coming of the Lord for the individual and for the community. Apostolic zeal and apostolic prudence need keen ears and open eyes. Such an attitude is impossible if morning, noon and night one's whole attention is absorbed by legal threats and the fear of hell because of innumerable positive laws. Moral instruction must teach constant vigilance in the service of the present hour which determines salvation. For this reason the fundamental lines of biblical morality must be clearly presented, especially the eschatological virtues of vigilance and of being prepared to respond to the call of inner grace and outward situation.

The auxiliary sciences of psychology and sociology must serve the same purpose. They will destroy the illusion of absolute freedom and lead to an appreciation of the true possibilities of the individual, due either to his psychological inheritance or to his social status. Similar considerations are applicable also to the community, which has its different historical possibilities. A morality of vigilance demands that the seminary education should not stress only juridical and legal matters, but that the auxiliary sciences should also be given a prominent place, because they teach one to appreciate the present situation. It does not suffice, however, only to make a place for sociology and psychology; they must be integrated into the whole presentation of morality.

There is no ideal manual of moral theology which could
have been written in 1250 and still be useful in 1970 or 5000.
Truly open to the needs of his time, St. Thomas Aquinas
sought a new system and a new manner of presentation. The
same is necessary today. And any future moral theologian will
have to think out anew what is most urgent in his particular
period and most capable of influencing his contemporaries. Of
course, revealed truth and fundamental biblical morality must
always be preserved, for example vigilance with regard to
the divinely given possibilities of doing good and spontaneous
obedience to the call of grace.

Sociological and psychological formation will facilitate
such an attitude, especially if they have been wisely integrated
into the whole moral education. They will teach the priest
always to be aware of the fluctuations of life.

Unless a synthesis with the social aspects of salvation is
sought such a morality of responsibility, initiative and spontaneity is dangerous, because it is constantly threatened by
the arbitrariness of unredeemed, selfish man. The Christian,
ever-valid, synthesis is spontaneity directed to social salvation.
In this respect Eph 4 and 1 Cor 12 can be considered as a
programme for moral instruction. Everyone is offered unique
chances, unique divine gifts and possibilities to serve his
neighbor and the community. The unique name by which
God calls us includes the duty to be active in the service of
salvation. We are not cogs in a machine, but living stones in
the temple of God. Every period of history has its special
possibilities, and within its community every individual person must look for his chances of development, especially in
the service of the whole. It is not sufficient to admit this
occasionally when teaching moral theology. The whole moral
instruction must be penetrated by it. This makes great de-

mands on the deepening and renewal of both the presentation and the general principles and indeed of the whole of casuistry. This must not proceed merely by deduction, but must teach that the ultimate question of conscience is concerned with the faithful response to a special call and the service of one's neighbor. It must teach a man to realize that reality in the service of God's kingdom is many-layered.

Our whole moral teaching must be characterized by the vision of the people of God on its journey to the final coming of the Lord. It is not a morality of individual Christians who may perhaps also look for a relation to the community in order to save themselves. It is definitely the morality of the people of God, and thus the morality of the individual within the whole. Through his moral instruction the future priest must learn to be first of all a good Christian that is a living member of the people of God. He will thus be helped to remain faithful to his special vocation. This will also prepare him to treat the laity as adults and to help them to become truly living members of the people of God. Future moral teaching in the seminaries will have to be profoundly influenced by the *Constitution on the Church,* especially by the chapters on the people of God and the perhaps even more important one on the position of the laity and their special vocation. This Constitution is so valuable that it will become of ever increasing usefulness for moral instruction. But it must be used at once, because we cannot afford to waste time.

In the moral manuals of the last century, at least in those of the legalistic "Roman" type, the world was only treated in the chapter on "Proximate Occasions of Sin." The Constitution of Vatican II on *The Church in the Modern World* will also be a milestone for future moral instruction. It is concerned with the cosmic aspect of redemption, the reverence for God's creation, for his action in history and the world, and it listens to the longing of creation for full participation in the freedom of the children of God. The responsibility for marriage and the family, cultural tasks, the passion for greater justice in economic and social life, the solidarity of the family of nations, the obligation of Christians to make the peace of Christ felt by their work for peace in the world: all these things will, in the future, be subjects of moral theology. The spirituality of the *Church in the Modern World* is determined by the mystery of the incarnation, the cross and the resurrection of Christ. We may well hope that, in the future, Catholic morality will be much more incarnational. The Christian can remain faithful to his vocation only if he is quite consciously the salt of the earth and the leaven in the mass.

The Second Vatican Council has initiated a courageous encounter with the world of today. It realizes, however, that this new attitude presupposes a deepening of the spirit of humility, self-denial and the cross of Christ. Undoubtedly moral theology will benefit much from the liturgical renewal, which places the paschal mystery, the redemption on the cross and the resurrection of Christ at its center. All the treatises of Christian moral teaching must be characterized by this mystery. They must make it clear that the Christian law is not in contradiction to or in competition with the Christian morality is itself part of the gospel, of the good news. A morality which is inspired by the paschal mystery will prepare man for great sacrifices, precisely because of the gospel and the glory of the risen Christ. All moral instruction must be inspired by the text: "The joy of the Lord is your strength" (Neh 8:10). If Christian morality is understood as the good news and is lived in Easter joy, it will also produce the joyful strength of the apostolic witness.

The apostolate is not mere technique nor mere activism. It must spring from a deep joy and a happily accepted vocation. Hence it is important that moral instruction in seminaries and therefore also moral preaching in Church and popular literature should be clearly united to the good news of the gospel centered in the resurrection and the glorious second coming of Christ.

The Christian community can be kept together and be effectively drawn to the apostolate not by controls in the confessional nor by the terrors of the Inquisition or similar psychological influences, but ultimately only by joy in the Lord. The Second Vatican Council has begun to demolish controls that have their origin in a spirit of fear and suspicion. This will certainly not diminish the effectiveness of the Church if it opens the way to more joyful preaching, to a happier life and a happier witness to the gospel.

Apostles are above all witnesses of the resurrection of Christ. This they can only be if they have really understood that the whole Christian life, including the Christian law, resides ultimately in the Easter joy and happy expectation of the return of the Lord. And this joy includes the cross of Christ.

"The law of Christ" is Christ himself and his love, Christ who lives in us until the end of time. The renewal of moral theology must follow the principle so solemnly pronounced by Pope Paul VI: "We know thee, Christ, alone." All moral teaching must announce Christ, must listen to Christ and help Christians and future priests to be more intimately united to Christ, in order to offer, in union with him, the redeeming love of one's neighbor to the Father. The law of Christ is the powerful love of Christ which urges us. It is not a law merely imposed from outside. It is no mere law of minimum demands.

It is the greatest power in the world and it causes us in all things to seek the salvation of our brothers and thus the glory of God. It is the bond of love which forges apostles, priests and laymen into the unity for which Christ implored the Father in his high-priestly prayer: "That they all may be one." The law of Christ demands responsibility to the highest degree: listening to the gospel, answering in the joyful worship of God, and listening also to that message which is given to us through the world crying out for redemption and through the need of our neighbor. Through the grace of the Holy Spirit this listening prepares us for the answer of redeeming love in and with Christ. Life according to the law of Christ means co-responsibility, that is union in the unique solidarity which has become visible to the world in Christ, his cross and his resurrection.

Nevertheless, all the people of God, every priest and every layman must know that they are only on the way to perfect listening and to perfect response. Their life will become an ever better response to the grace of God only if they listen to each other and share their burden and responsibility. In the spirit of Vatican II we priests and moral theologians are becoming increasingly conscious of the fact that our humble listening to the voice of the laity, to their experience and their needs, is part of our constant conversion. This will make it easier also for the layman to listen to the teaching Church which he encounters in the humble service of the priest.

4

THE DYNAMIC OF THE CHRISTIAN LIFE

At a time of restoration, when the generally accepted ideal was "preservation and continuity all along the line" it was understandable that Christian morality, too, was presented mainly as constant, tending merely to remain the same. The principal characteristic of our own time is the dynamic of constant progress in almost all departments of science and technology. New discoveries are being made every day, and the pace of evolution increases from one year to the other.

Christian morality, however, is even more dynamic, not only now but at all times. It ought to seem strange to the men of the twentieth century when moralists present the doctrine of the Christian life in a merely static way. Such a presentation risks tempting the Christian to self-satisfied smugness, an attitude censured by Christ more severely than almost any other. A deliberately dynamic presentation of Christian morality corresponds both to the spirit of our times and especially to a life according to the spiritual law in Christ Jesus.

The source of Christian morality is the victory of Christ in the fullness of time, even though this victory has not yet become everywhere evident. The history between the first and the second coming of the Lord is filled with the dynamic of the paschal mystery and the expectation of the blessed return of our Lord. The Christian expectation that looks forward to the final fulfillment draws its force from the fullness of salvation that is already present. The grace active in the present is the dynamic of Christian hope. Though Christian life means hoping for the coming of the Lord, this hope must always be related to the other truth that the Lord has already come and remains with us. Our Lord himself urges us by his partly hidden and yet in other respects open presence to direct our whole life to his ultimate coming.

The essence of Christian hope has often been misunderstood under the influence of a mercenary spirit according to which the present life consisted mainly in collecting merits under the oppressive burden of external laws, while eschatology meant the reward in the next world for works performed here on earth. But Christian morality is joyful if we have a proper theological understanding of its eschatological character. For it implies the knowledge that we are redeemed, justified and sanctified. We have the absolute confidence of faith that Christ has won the victory once and for all, and that everyone who lives in Christ is sure of victory. Hence Christian morality does not only look to the Lord who has ascended into heaven from where he will return. It also looks to the cross as the great sign of love which radiates the splendor of the resurrection. Christian life means following the Lord, who has sent us his Spirit and is himself our way.

The eschatological character of Christian morality, on the other hand, signifies the consciousness of living in a "meantime." It is a time of the fullness of grace, but it is also a time of separation, in which the enemies of Christ, knowing that their time is short, do all they can to deprive us of our share in the victory of Christ. The time of separation allows neither idleness nor rest.

The Church sees itself as the new Israel on the way through the desert to the heavenly Jerusalem. Now if even the Israel according to the flesh was comforted and encouraged by the presence of the Lord in a pillar of fire, how much

more the new Israel, which is assured of the constant presence of the Lord: "Moving forward through trial and tribula-
tion, the Church is strengthened by the power of God's grace
promised to her by the Lord, so that in the weakness of the
flesh she may not waver from perfect fidelity, but remain a
bride worthy of her Lord; that moved by the Holy Spirit she
may never cease to renew herself, until through the cross she
arrives at the light which knows no setting."[1] The Church
knows herself to be the holy people of God, but she also prays
every day: "Forgive us our trespasses." The people of God
knows, therefore, that it needs daily to be purified and to go
on striving. The presence of the Lord is dynamic, he is calling
and leading the Church. The redeeming and sanctifying presence of the risen Lord is a powerful invitation to his people
to look forward and to prepare for his final coming by heeding
the present hour.

Hence the dynamic of Christian morality does not primarily derive from man, from his efforts or from his merits.
The dynamic is not the result of merely human activity and
hope. It derives essentially from God, who is constantly active
in his grace and revelation.

In the Council discussions about the original draft on the
two sources of revelation there was a violent clash between
those who regarded revelation almost exclusively as static,
and the majority of the Fathers who saw it in a personal and
dynamic way. Revelation is no mere communication of ideas
and cannot be compared with a system of abstract philosophical notions. Nor does it aim at a mere contemplation of ideas.
Revelation is a powerful act of God, in whom word and deed
are the same. Where God speaks, something happens, salva-

---

1. **Constitution on the Church,** No. 9; cf. nos. 48-51.

tion takes place. God's revelation approaches man in his saving deeds. Revelation itself is essentially the powerful claim of love that moves man to an active response. In revelation God communicates himself to man and gives him the power to open himself and to surrender.

In the Scriptures this dynamic characteristic of revelation is expressed especially when they speak of the glory of God, of the message of joy in the Lord and of grace.

Holy Scripture does not describe the worship of God so much as a virtue or inner quality of man. It appears rather as the action of God himself who reveals dynamically the splendor of his glory. We are thinking here especially of the biblical concepts of *Kebod Yahweh* (the glory of the Lord), *kadosh* (the holiness of God) and *shem Yahweh* (the name of God).

Hence, in the Bible, worship or adoration (*Anbetung*) does not begin with man. We are confronted by the God who reveals himself, and whose self-revelation is powerful. It forces man, the miserable sinner, to his knees and causes him to tremble. Man trembles before God's over-powering sanctity revealed in his saving actions or in the works of creation. The same revelation, however, causes man, the friend of God, to rejoice, it fills him with a happiness which turns his whole life into a praise of glory.

This dynamic revelation of the glory of God, of the name and of the holiness of God is the true basis of the worship that is at the center of biblical morality.

Hence revelation itself produces man's response of reverent and joyful adoration. It is no mere imperative that comes from God: "You shall worship the Lord your God, and him only shall you serve." God does not only teach man what he is to do. God reveals himself, and with his divine presence and power he impels man to worship him. This, of course, includes an obligation; on the other hand it is possible for man to refuse.

God's revelation is an external event and at the same time a powerful interior call. The dynamic, therefore, is not only due to the eternal event of God's self-revelation but also to an interior call. In other words: God's revelation, which also appears externally, is a call addressed to the whole man, coming directly from the holiness and love of God.

It is a rewarding task to work through the whole of the Old and New Testament from this single point of view of the love of God revealing itself, which wants to make man a humble and joyful worshipper. The splendor of Yahweh shines forth in the cloud, which is both light and dark, which goes before the people in the wilderness. On Mount Sinai the glory of God appears as fire which gives the people a salutary fright because of its sinfulness. The glory of Yahweh fills the temple (Ex 40:35; 1 Kings 8:11). One of the most beautiful texts on the subject is Ex 33: Moses cannot see the face of God directly without dying. He sees only God's back, from afar, and yet this causes his own face to shine to strongly that Aaron and the people of Israel cannot bear the reflection of God's holiness in the face of Moses (Ex 33:22). God shows forth his holiness in the works of creation as well as in the marvellous deeds in which he reveals himself to his people as their salvation (Num 14:22; Is 35:2; 40:5). St. Paul actually piles one word on the other in order to describe the power of God's glory as it reveals itself: "May you be strengthened with all power, according to his glorious might, for all endurance and patience, with joy, giving thanks to the Father, who has qualified us to share in the inheritance of the saints in light" (Col 1:11f; cf. Eph 1:19; 6:10).

4

God's revelation is a source of life and a purifying fire. The dynamic can be represented as a harmony of contrasts (Rudolf Otto), the tension between holy fear and exuberant joy producing not only individual acts of worship, but a completely new life. The revelation of God's holiness causes man to cry out: "Depart from me, for I am a sinful man, O Lord" (Lk 5:8); but these words include also an urgent approach to the Lord. His revelation brings comfort and joy: "Lord, remain with us." Peter, who humbly confesses himself to be a sinner when he sees the miracles of the Lord, is wild with joy before the revelation in Jesus Christ which far surpasses the revelations of God in Moses and Elijah: "Let us make three booths" (Lk 9:28-36).

Nothing is so evident in all biblical descriptions of the revelation of God as the primacy of God's own action and grace. Hence the apostles do not speak as philosophers. They do not develop an abstract system, but are witnesses of God's revelation: "We have beheld his glory, glory as of the only Son from the Father" (Jn 1:14).

It is quite impossible to present Christian morality divorced from the good news of life in Christ Jesus. Christian ethics must not be added, as it were, to the gospel. Christian morality presented as a mere doctrine of norms makes it futile in the sense that the actually dynamic element is taken out of the message, even if it is not denied. The gospels make it absolutely clear that Christ is not a moralist. He does not preach morality apart from his message of joy, but he preaches the renewal of the heart through the good news of the time of salvation, when God himself will renew men's hearts. The moral imperative: "Renew your hearts" is contained in the good news and is inseparable from the call: "Believe in the gospel" (Mk 1:15). Morality is an integral part of the gospel, which approaches us in Christ himself, in his Person, his saving actions and his words. Christ preaches the good news and with it the new way of salvation, above all by giving himself. He is both messenger and message. He always announces his gospel in the Church, and with the gospel his way of life. Christian morality means life in Christ Jesus. Hence the fundamental demand made on us with this greatest message is that we should remain in him and that his word should remain in us. The Christian must always be conscious that the impulse for a truly Christian life does not come from a mere law but from Christ who is living in him and wants an ever greater living space within him.

Christian morality led to a joyless Christianity when, by reason of technical simplification and the influence of a legalistic spirit it submerged the Christian under a flood of imperatives and casuistic solutions. Paul Claudel describes the attitude of the Christian who groans under a purely legalistic morality divorced from the gospel by making him say: "True, we love Christ, but nothing in the world can induce us to love morality."

The Christian who is guided merely by moral rules inevitably resembles a man who has looked at his natural face in a mirror and then goes away and forgets what he looked like. Only a man who looks at the perfect law of freedom and remains in it will be a doer of acts and "be blessed in his doing" (Jas 1:23-25).

Both in the lecture room and in the pulpit morality can be renewed only by a more living contact with the mystery of Christ and salvation history enacted in ourselves. As an integrated part of the gospel message morality "should show the nobility of the Christian vocation of the faithful."[2] Hence this renewal demanded by the Council brings morality again into direct contact with the gospel and thus gives back to it the urgent power of salvation.

The Jews had returned from the exile and were rebuilding Jerusalem under great difficulties, having to defend themselves against attack all the time. Then the priest Ezra called a meeting and read the Book of the Covenant before all the people, producing a profound contrition and change of mind. In this situation the priest Ezra spoke the well-known words: "The joy of the Lord is your strength" (Neh 8:10). So the Old Testament already gives us the key to the dynamic morality of the people of the covenant.

This becomes even more obvious in the New Testament. Even the first summary of Christ's manner of preaching in the "Urevangelium" (Mk 1:14f), makes evident the unity between the gospel message and the call to repentance: "Repent and believe in the gospel."

Matthew's synthesis of the preaching of the new law in the Sermon on the Mount begins with the ninefold: "Blessed are. . . ." Nine is the number of perfection. The infinitely blessed triune God gives the hearers and doers of the gospel a share in his life of bliss. In his shortened presentation of the Sermon on the Mount, Luke (6:22f) has a fourfold "Blessed." For him, too, to be blessed is the essence of completeness; in the sphere of Greek civilization it is the fullness of fundamental attitudes. John introduces his great sythesis of the new law: "Love one another, even as I have loved you" with the words: "Having loved his own . . . he loved them to

---

2. **Decree on Priestly Formation,** No. 16.

the end." Immediately before proclaiming the law the Lord pronounces joy to be part of it: "These things I have spoken to you, that my joy may be in you, and that your joy may be full."

Some moralists ought to be told the same as the German poet Friedrich Schiller told the philosopher Immanuel Kant: "I should like to serve my friends, but alas, I do it with pleasure." Exponents of rigoristic and legalistic thought believe that they serve morality best if they produce as complete a code of duties as possible, hedged round with numerous threats. But those who know the heart of man know also that the best effects are not produced by a jejune doctrine of duties, but by the moral message contained in the good news of the gospel. The law of faith is wholly contained in the gospel message and is, indeed, this very message. This law does not destroy the moral law, but provides its dynamic foundation. Only if morality wholly expresses the blessed covenant will the Christian feel in his heart and proclaim: "Lord, your law is my delight" (Ps 118 (119)).

A legalistically inclined student may be disoriented by mild attitudes which derive from a deep understanding of man's weakness and pilgrim state. But for Christians who are at home in a truly evangelical morality, which is integrated with the gospel message, gentleness and understanding will be another dynamic spur to increasing faithfulness.

Those who are living in conditions unworthy of men will only become more embittered and rebel if they are threatened with jail for if a man's whole life is a kind of jail he will not fear imprisonment. It is the same with moral teaching. If it is only a collection of hard imperatives with a thousand possibilities of going to hell, this will not seem to be such a fearful threat at the end. But if the Christian understands the happiness and honor of Christ's friendship and the beauty of the Christian way of life, he will have a powerful incentive to avoid even a venial sin. If he sees that love itself warns him against sin and hell, and that hell is the permanent "No" to the blessed love of God, holy fear together with blissful love will be a powerful bulwark against sin.

In the Second Part of his *Summa Theologica,* St. Thomas treats of grace, and in connection with this of the new law, thus following the fundamental biblical line. Typical moralism begins with the commandments and speaks of grace chiefly or exclusively as a means to keep the commandments. In this case the main difference between the Old and the New Covenant would be this, that Old Testament man would have had the law, but not sufficient grace, whereas the man of the New Covenant would now have the means to fulfill that law. Such a presentation is not only legalistic, but also anthropocentric. It reduces not only grace, but also the Redeemer himself to a means of keeping the law, thus being assured of the reward, at least in accordance with the mentality of such moralistic handbooks. But the main concern of both the Old and the New Covenant is not the "you shall" or "you shall not." The main concern is the covenant, while the law is its expression. God's nearness is the fundamental fact, from which results the impulse to surrender oneself to him.

We do not oppose the notional differentiation between sanctifying and actual grace. But the theological system, too, must express the unity of both. Grace is the dynamic presence of Christ in the power of the Holy Spirit. It communicates and increases the divine life in us. Grace is the bond of the covenant. It unites us in the most intimate friendship with the

Lord and his people, or, better, the Lord himself unites us
to himself and his disciples in grace.

Grace is a powerful revelation of God's love in the hearts
of the redeemed. Thus grace must be considered essentially as
ordered to glory. Grace is that inner urging of God's love
through which the external, visible revelation produces our
salvation. Of its very nature grace urges us to become conscious of the gracious presence of God. It invites us to see
God himself at work, to adore him and to follow the dynamic
of his self-revelation through all our actions.

Both sanctifying and actual grace are a beginning and
germ of eternal life. Now this is to be understood as a shin-
ing forth in the glory of Christ and a praise of God's majesty.
Hence we are urged by the very nature of grace, or, better,
by the glorified Christ in the Holy Spirit, to show forth in our
life the action of grace for the honor and glory of God.

Grace is participation in the paschal mystery, in which
the Son and the Heavenly Father glorify each other. Thus
grace prepares us for a life in Christ Jesus in which we die to
our own glory and tend only to the glory of God, expecting
that God will give us a share in the glory of Christ.

The incarnate Word has glorified the Father in his flesh,
and his glory shines forth in his glorified body. Grace includes
the redemption of the body as well as of the soul. Hence it
impels us to renew not only our inner thought and feeling, but
also our bodily actions.

Grace, therefore, is the most powerful energy that approaches us in Christ Jesus. It unites us to the love with which
the Son has loved the Father and his human brothers. Grace
itself is the love of Christ which urges us (2 Cor 5:14). Grace
impels us to look upon the crucified and glorified Christ, who

is glorified because of his active love. Thus grace unites us to Christ and spurs us on to devote our whole life to the loving adoration and the adoring love of God, in which we love one another in, and for the sake of our common Lord.

Grace is the dynamic presence of the Holy Spirit. Sanctifying grace is the dynamic indwelling of the Holy Spirit in us, a presence which, in the hour of salvation, becomes the powerful impulse of actual grace. There is, however, also an actual grace which only prepares the indwelling of the Holy Spirit in his sanctified temple; it is the dynamic of a presence which wants to lead to intimate union.

To sum up: The Holy Spirit within us bears witness to our spirit that we are children of God, co-heirs with Christ, "provided we suffer with him in order that we may also be glorified with him" (Rom 8:16f). The dynamic is perhaps best expressed if we follow Thomas Aquinas in regarding the Holy Spirit himself as the new law, as him who works in us the love that is the fulfillment of the law. The external presentation of the law being wholly ordered to the dynamic of the Holy Spirit, it shares, as the good news of the new life, in the dynamic of the Spirit's law of life in Christ Jesus.

The dynamic of the Christian life which corresponds to the reality of grace is also expressed in the gospel parable of the talents (Mt 25:14-30). Not all receive the same measure. God is generous to all, but without limiting his generosity. He expects the talents he gives to men to bear fruit, to double. God is love, but he is also the Lord. If he gives love he does not discard his glory. The love which man receives is the gift of the all-holy God, hence it involves responsibility. But this responsibility should not first be regarded as a threat of judgment, but as the inner fruitfulness which belongs to the gifts of the Holy Spirit. Christian life should bring fruit in joy, in goodness and in love. But its measure is no mere external minimum law. The measure of fruitfulness is the measure of grace.

A morality that follows the New Testament image of the talents makes man humble. He regards himself as nothing, yet as rich, in order to give all back to the Lord.

Christian life is generous, but the Christian does not imagine that he has something of his own to give to God. Christian generosity is humble. When the Christian has done everything according to the grace given to him, he knows truly that all is grace.

The Christian living under the new law cannot be content with an external keeping of the law. His true standard is the love of God, as it has been revealed to us in the paschal mystery and been communicated individually through God's natural and supernatural gifts. That Christian existence is a gift is not an invitation to a certain Quietism, but the holy rule of the gospel which urges us on.

General laws are minimum laws, they are necessary to point the way for the sinner who has lost his direction, for the man in the purgative way. For the true Christian it becomes a real rule of life only in full unity with the gifts of grace.

There can be no doubt that God judges us in accordance with the graces he has given us. For this reason it is clear that the borderlines between imperfection, venial sin and mortal sin cannot be exactly the same for all men. Mortal sin and venial sin differ like hell differs from purgatory, but purgatory is a temporary, even if painful, transition to heaven. It is impossible to explain the difference between mortal and venial sin as a mere difference of degree, a difference of "matter," of the object of the commandment. The difference concerns ultimately even though not exclusively, the degree of insight and of freedom. The external object is only the impulse that calls forth the use of insight and freedom. The man who has been given more will realize that his "No" is ultimately a "No" to the love of God, who gives and demands, even if it is a question of relatively minor matters.

A merely static understanding of the difference between mortal and venial sin will discourage the beginner who has come from afar, while it will make the man to whom much is given lazy and impertinent, if he is only concerned with the external minimum law. The biblical view of a morality of gifts also corresponds better to the insights of psychology, which explains the limits of value judgments and freedom and makes us see all human life as a development marked by struggle, progress and occasional setbacks. A merely static morality which only considers the external law has already been described in the ancient myth of Procrustes. Procrustes invited his guests in order to fit them all into his standard size bed. If one was too long, he cut off his legs and his head; if one was too small, he stretched his limbs until they filled his bed. Every morning there were obsequies. The morality of the gifts of grace is gentle, yet it constantly urges men to make progress. Such morality also makes us humble in our judgments of others, for God alone knows the measure of his gifts.

A morality of gifts does not at all undermine the validity of the external law, which, on the contrary, is enlivened by it. It is nevertheless obvious that a morality of talents does not place the emphasis on the definition of minimum laws, but, like the Sermon on the Mount and the farewell speeches of Christ, stresses especially the Christian ideals and subjects the individual laws to the law of perfection.

A detailed morality completely based on laws of limitation

or minute rulings is necessarily static and non-dynamic. But if these laws are integrated in the great commandment: "LOVE one another, even as I have loved you," they, too, will become dynamic, because they are related to the gift of grace.

The representatives of a dynamic view of Christian morality like for example J. M. Sailer, J. B. Hirscher and M. Jocham, give a central place to the chapter on the first and second conversion. The representatives of the so-called "Roman type" of morality, on the other hand, who present the whole Christian life from the point of view of the external law, do not have a special treatise on conversion. There can be no doubt that in biblical and patristic teaching the doctrine of constant conversion is given a place of honor. The Benedictine monk is an ideal of the Christian precisely because of his vow of *"conversio continua,"* continuous conversion. This means that the Christian must never become self-satisfied after his fundamental conversion of the "first justification." He must know that his participation in the life of Christ impels him to constant growth. But for the Christian growth is possible only through a struggle with the concupiscence of the old, selfish man.

The second or continual conversion makes it impossible to hold that it is normal for a Christian to relapse frequently into the state of mortal sin. Both the gospels and the preaching and letters of the apostles are full of optimism, that is, of the God-given confidence that nothing can separate the Christian from the love of Christ. The dynamic of the Christian life is destroyed or at least greatly disturbed if we speak too easily of mortal sin in connection with relatively unimportant external commandments. We were horrified to find in five still widely used handbooks of moral theology that their authors, taken together, still present about two hundred legal prescriptions of the Church as occasions for mortal sin, whereas they find only about ninety occasions of venial sin in these and similar prescriptions. A priest who knew all these five manuals and wanted to save his soul would have to concentrate his whole energy on these questions, which would leave him little strength for Christian enthusiasm and for listening to the call of grace. Though there is an efficacious dynamic of fear if eternal hell is threatened for relatively minor offences such as leaving out one of the little hours of the breviary, nevertheless where it exists the true dynamic of Christian love and joy will be absent. The law itself will not be attractive if it is presented in such a way, but will rather be the occasion of transgression and of a hostile attitude. If a man is primarily impelled and instructed by the good news of the gospel on the other hand, he will also recognize the true meaning of the external laws of the Church and keep them gladly.

The tremendous dynamic of Christian morality is not only expressed by the parable of the talents, but also by the New Testament notion of the *kairós,* the hour of grace. The life of our Lord himself is presented as a waiting for the hour determined by the Father. This hour is primarily his passion, death and resurrection, and it gives a powerful dynamic also to every other hour of his life. All these other hours anticipate the final hour and prepare him for it. The chapters of St. John's Gospel which are a synthesis of Christ's moral preaching are introduced by the words: "Now before the feast of the Passover, when Jesus knew that his hour had come" (Jn 13:1). The new law, "Love one another as I have loved you," is promulgated in view of the great time of salvation between the first and the second coming of the Lord, and thus also in view of that hour of grace.

In Holy Scripture the Church is presented under the image

of the virgins who keep the oil in their lamps, always watching for the coming of the Bridegroom (cf. Mt 25:13). The hour of the coming of the Bridegroom is not only the Second Coming, but also every hour of grace, every salvific situation prepared by God. Everyone of these hours or moments is unique. It contains the energies of the paschal mystery and prepares us for our encounter with the Lord in his second coming.

In the light of the biblical teaching on the hour of salvation, the eschatological virtues of vigilance and hope receive a special importance. Their dynamic character becomes immediately evident. Watchfulness is the response to the present energies which the Creator and Savior instills into our seemingly very weak life. Not only individuals but the whole Christian community must practice vigilance. Both individually and in common, Christians must search for the signs of the time.

Pope John as well as Pope Paul have often spoken of the need to observe the signs of the time, and this has also become a characteristic of Vatican II. It is summarized in the *Pastoral Constitution on the Church in the Modern World.* God is not presented as having created the world six thousand — or millions of — years ago, furnished it with rules and commandments and then left it more or less to itself. The doctrine of creation places us here and now before the Creator who is acting continually. For the eye of faith of the humbly watchful Christian the events of world history become an encounter with the Creator and Savior and a present call of God. Salvation happens in the heart of history. Thus the Christian is always confronted by the powerful action of the Word of God.

The Council *Decree on Priestly Formation* enjoins on all teachers of theology, but especially on those of moral theology,

to make more living contact with salvation history; we ought
therefore to concentrate especially on the marvellously fruitful biblical doctrine of the *kairós,* the signs of the time, the
watchful virgins.

The biblical ethic of watching for the hour of grace does
not diminish the importance of the law. The vigilant Christian knows the goal of his life through his interior conscience
as well as through the external law. And for this very reason
he investigates all possible routes.

A merely static presentation of Christian morality is always
a legalistic morality, in which the permanent evangelical
teaching is not distinguished from the transitory legal prescriptions of the past. Because of this failure to distinguish,
Christians are burdened with many transitory forms which
were, indeed, important in the past, but which now hinder
the progress of the Church of Vatican II, greatly trusting in
God, is beginning to adapt its law to the present hour of salvation, hence it would be catastrophic if its moral teaching
were still to be mainly a presentation of positive injunctions
and failed to stress the permanent characteristics of Christian
morality. There will be a thorough reform of the law, in
accordance with the signs of the time, hence many priests of
the old school and the laymen instructed by them will have
doubts and ask whether the whole morality has changed.

Time and again we encounter the question, whether or
not it is asked openly: "Is not such a view of Christian morality too dangerous?" Indeed, a static presentation of moral
theology does not only reflect the image of the past, but also
the attempt to protect oneself from surprises by over-bold
Christians through insisting on merely external norms.

It must be admitted quite frankly that a dynamic view
of morality has its dangers, indeed, it is a very great risk. But

just because this risk is so great the Christian will realize that he cannot bear it alone. The dynamic view of morality forces the Christian to surrender himself completely to God's guidance on the way of salvation. It is the risk to accompany Christ on the way of the cross, to lose his life in the hope of finding it again in the Lord. This is not human wisdom. What is too great a risk from the human point of view, is wisdom with God, which presupposes the perfect knowledge of human weakness. It is the wisdom of the cross but also trusting faith in the resurrection of Christ. The Christian life is essentially a risk, of which we become aware in the mystery of Easter. This life is guided by the principles of the New Testament; in it a man surrenders to the Holy Spirit as his true law. Servile fear has no place in it, if a man surrenders himself to God and expects all from him, he is freed from *Angst* (anxiety or dread), which receives its power from human egoism.

The true danger of the Christian is selfishness. This shows itself in just that fearful attitude which wants to secure everything with external controls and prescriptions. This fear is present not only in superiors, but as often and perhaps even more often in subjects as well who would rather hide behind external laws and seek their own satisfaction in their observance.

Many Christians have been disturbed by the events of Vatican II, for example by the reform of the liturgy, and ask again and again whether it is to be hoped that after the Council there will once more be a final and unchangeable order. In view of the experience that the risen Christ is near to his Church and gives it such fullness of life it is frightening that there are Christians who are not only sleeping guards at the tomb of Christ, but that there are those who would even try to imprison him again in the grave of their beloved formulas.

5

A CONTEMPORARY VIEW OF THE ASCETICAL LIFE

Despite the diversity of views within the Catholic Church, the Council has made an extraordinary contribution to the emergence of certain common perspectives, especially in the *Constitution on the Church* (Chapter V: "The Call of the Whole Church to Holiness"). In this sense we outline the principles of the spiritual life.

On the thirteenth Sunday after Pentecost the Church prays: "Almighty and everlasting God, grant us an increase of faith, hope and charity, and that we may deserve to obtain what you promise, make us love what you command." This prayer expresses the classic view of the spiritual life. The emphasis lies on the truth that God takes the initiative and that we receive everything from him.

Thus faith is not so much described as a virtue of man or a quality of the soul as in Aristotelian thought, but is seen primarily in the light of God's self-revelation. Faith is dialogue, begun by God himself. Revealing himself, he opens the heart of man. God glorifies his truth by giving men a share in it. Thus we may describe faith as the grateful and joyous acceptance of the truth of salvation, while always being conscious that Christ himself is this truth. Thus faith is a grateful response to the redemption of Christ who heals us in truth.

Our life, therefore, is under the law of faith. Gospel and law are not opposed to each other. The glad tidings in Christ is the fundamental law of faith; faith itself is the great return, the great conversion: "Repent, and believe in the gospel" (Mk 1:15).

Life under the law of faith is praise of God and his saving truth. Faith has its place in life (*Sitz im Leben*) first of all in the celebration of the mystery of salvation; there Christ speaks to his bride, there he announces the gospel. The bride of Christ, the community of the faithful, responds in faith and praise. The mystery, however, does not stand outside of life, but must determine its fundamental form. This means that the whole Christian life is seen as a joyous and grateful listening to God who speaks to us in Christ, and in all events of our life. Thus our whole life will be a response of faith, and all will ultimately be seen in the purifying light of this saving mystery.

"Grant us an increase of hope": hope is not to be understood as human desire. God himself wants men to share in his blessed love and tells them: "I am the salvation of my people." Hope is the gift of God's redeeming love. It receives its power not so much from our desire for blessedness as from the will of God to make us blessed. Christian hope not only looks forward to things to come, it is always also a praising and grateful affirmation of the present hour of salvation, expressing the fullness of eschatological time.

This fullness of salvation, however, is not yet fully revealed. Thus faith and hope are essentially related to growth. They are the tension between what is already there and what is not yet present, but the present measure of salvation powerfully impels us to grow and to look forward to the perfect revelation of the blessed freedom of the children of God.

"Grant us an increase of love." Love in the Christian sense is not to be understood as our own achievement, but as the love with which God has loved us first and enabled us to love him also in Christ. God glorifies himself in the love which he pours forth in our hearts through the Holy Spirit. God is love, his love is the dialogue between the divine Persons, in which he wants man to share. For the Christian love of God and neighbor is no mere means to get to heaven. The love that comes from God is the dialogue I – you – we. Our brother is included in the love God has for us and we for him. For God loves me and you, us, his family, his chosen people in one and the same love.

To love God means also to love his commandments, which are the expression of his love and point to perfect love. Hence we grow in love by keeping his commandments ever more joyfully through achieving a synthesis of all moral life in the basic theme of love. A love which is not identified with one's own perfection and which does not use God as a means, such a love prays by the very way a man lives: "What can I give to the Lord for all he has done for me." Faith, hope and love are essentially the worship of the holy God who sanctifies us.

Besides emphasizing the character of service of the ministry and indeed of the whole Christian life the theologians of the Second Vatican Council seem to have been most concerned to achieve a synthesis. The synthesis between the celebration of the mystery and the conduct of one's life, between gospel and law is decisive for the understanding of Christian morality. This synthesis presents itself as "life in Christ Jesus." Paul expresses this synthesis in the "law of faith," the "law of grace," the "law of Christ."

By solemnly teaching the general vocation to holiness which consists essentially in the love of God and one's neighbor, the Council has made it impossible to separate morality from asceticism. The ascetical effort is not something else beside morality, but emphasizes an essential feature of Christian morality, that is to say the law of growth, the constant necessity of effort, purification and self-examination.

According to the Gospel there are two basic forms of a personalist conception of the world. Both emphasize the value of the human person, but are in the last analysis completely opposed to each other.

The adamitic (*adamitisch*) personalism regards man and everything else only insofar as they serve its own glory or its desire for happiness. All else is considered only as a means. Adam wants to be wise through himself, he wants a part of freedom which he does not receive from God, he seeks life in himself. Adamitic personalism largely expresses itself in Aristotelian thought which imprisons the moral ethos in the categories of end and means. The Stoic ethic, too, is ultimately an Adamitic ethic; it does not, indeed, deny God and one's neighbor, but they are chiefly related to the perfection of self.

The Buddhist, anxious to free himself from the unrest of man's desire for life, does not find his Thou either, but remains thrown back on the ego, regardless of whether he relates this to perfect emptiness or ultimate fulfillment.

Pharisaism, which uses God's law as a means of self-righteousness, is a classical embodiment of egocentric personalism, even if it constantly speaks of God and his law.

It is a characteristic of adamitic personalism that its egocentric attitude hides the Thou or at least causes it to take second place. The Protestant theologian Tersteegen expressed a profound Christian experience when he wrote that looking at the self makes a man ill, while looking at the Thou brings health. The triune life of God is wholly concerned with the Thou. The Father is wholly himself by giving all his power, wisdom and love to his Son; the Son is wholly himself by receiving himself from, and giving himself back to the Father. The holy Spirit is the gift, the bond of love.

The Christian personalist finds his true self in looking to Christ, for thus he sees himself loved by him who is love in person.

In the last twenty-five years Catholic thinkers have been greatly occupied by biblical personalism such as it has been developed by the Austrian Catholic school teacher Ferdinand Ebner (d. 1931) and the Jewish theologian Martin Buber (d. 1965). What is best in Catholic and Protestant thought meet in this personalism of "I-thou-we." With regard to God this personalism means: All I am and have is a word of God's love. Hence I can find my true "I" only by listening to God, in a life which becomes wholly the response of gratitude and love. God calls every man by an ineffable, unique name which cannot be exchanged; but this name can be found only in the dialogue of adoring and trusting love with God.

God calls each one of us directly into existence. Through his creative word he gives man individuality and personality. But he wants a man fully to awaken and to realize his name only through the message of love that passes through his neighbor. Hence we cannot find our blissful Thou in God unless we concern ourselves with God's beloved messengers. No one realizes his proper name if he uses his neighbor merely as a means to perfect himself. A man gains the authentic, healing experience of his "I" only if he is open for the Thou, for the dignity, uniqueness and needs of his neighbor.

The best experience of the "I" is given by looking at the Thou, the Thou of God in community with one's brother.

In the heart of the Christian, Adamitic and Christian personalism fight against each other. Hence we must examine whether our life is truly directed to the Thou of God and our neighbor so that we can find our genuine "I." The ascetical examination of conscience is concerned with the self-realization of the "I," but not under the aspect of self-perfection or self-redemption, but of the great question whether I am really quite open for God and my neighbor. In checking on himself the Christian is neither self-destructive nor closed in on himself. Such self-examination is rather a striving for deeper faith as a hearing and answering. It is a way of hope by which man surrenders to God, a way of love by which man glorifies God by his selfless service of his neighbor and the community. Thus self-examination belongs to the worship of God and the service of one's brothers, for it sees all questions of detail in the light of the great reality of the love of God and neighbor.

Self-examination and all other ascetical practices must serve life, and both must be in the right proportion to each other. But there is the danger that life, that is to say openness to God and one's neighbor, may be subordinated to self-centered asceticism. This reflexive, self-examining attitude may diminish spontaneous openness to the Thou if one's fundamental concern is the perfection of self.

There is an asceticism of a multiplicity of individual practices and austerities which become more or less an end in themselves. Thus asceticism may become a flight from life and its true duties. Christian asceticism must above all correspond to life. This means that self-denial must be integrated into a life of worshipful love of God and loving service of one's neighbor, looking towards the blessed liberty of the children of God. This means being free for God and one's neighbor, from which one's own self receives its fullness.

Christian life must chiefly be practiced in an ever fuller encounter with God and one's neighbor. But apart from this it must also be a preparation for the great events of life. There must be forethought, and there must also be examination afterwards.

Self-examination before acting is determined by the "discernment of spirits." This great Christian tradition is especially developed in Benedictine spirituality. A truly traditional Christian morality places the chief emphasis not on casuistry but on the signs by which to discern the spirits. Such a sign, among others, is peace of soul. If an impulse, a desire or a plan increases one's peace of soul, furthers prayer and brings joy, then it may be assumed that they are from God.

A further basic sign is one's response to the individual gifts of grace, the special opportunities for doing good which God has prepared, especially with regard to serving one's neighbor and the community, to building up the mystical body of Christ. Christian casuistry, too, must be practiced in this spirit, the same as that in which Paul solved the question of those who were strong and enlightened, e.g., in Rom 14 and 15 and in 1 Cor 4.

It is ultimately the question of how our actions affect the salvation of others. Thus the service of salvation is not subordinated to the desire for one's own blessedness; if we have truly the spirit of God we shall see our own eternal happiness as a fruit of serving the salvation of our neighbor. The philosopher Max Scheler expresses this thought of Christian ascetics when he says that the true personal value of the enrichment of the self comes "on the back of action" (auf dem Rücken der Handlung). Action is seen essentially as an answer to values, as true dialogue.

Self-examination produces a special positive resolution. True, Christian life must be a spontaneous answer to the possibilities God prepares at a certain moment. But it would be naive to imagine that this spontaneity is possible without a conscious resolution. For the spirit of vigilance must be accompanied also by the conscious striving for purification and growth. Christian ascetical teachers have always emphasized the paramount importance of a firm resolution, especially in connection with the sacrament of penance. This, however, must not be arbitrary but must be the fruit of an authentically Christian self-examination. Thus it will always aim at a greater openness to God and a better service of one's neighbor and of the community.

From time to time the Christian must look back and examine from what motives he has acted and what effects his actions have had on his neighbor and the community. He must find out whether his actions and aspirations have advanced his interior availability for God and his fellowmen. If the Christian has accustomed himself to examine himself periodically, he will find it easier to realize when his concern has not been for God and his neighbor. One of the fundamental rules of Christian asceticism is the necessity to admit at once in the depth of our heart if we have not used God's grace and the opportunities for doing good or have actually done evil. Evil means a rejection of the value calling us and ultimately of the Person representing this call. Self-examination is the way to a new encounter in the spirit of humility and contrition. The Christian should often ask for the grace to arrive as soon as possible at contrition and the renewal of his resolution once he has sinned. For every sin, that is to say every rejection of the invitation to love, causes the whole person to deteriorate unless it is followed immediately by humble contrition and renewed love. Contrition means personal encounter with God who recalls us in his mercy. It is a renewed "Yes," and so also expresses our confidence in the mercy of God and our humble praise.

We will now consider what has so far been said in the light of the sacrament of penance. A sacrament provides a personal encounter with Christ, who is the principal agent, while human action is response made possible by grace. In the sacrament of penance the Lord looks back in mercy on man's failure and absolves in view of his continual conversion. In this sacrament man meets Christ, consciously looking at him and at himself only with the eyes of Christ, hence it is the true way to being freed from Adamitic personalism into redeemed personalism. Christ's healing action in the sacrament of penance is at the same time sanctifying. Thus the Christian, consoled and freed by the mercy of the Lord, is joined to him by gratitude. His further desire of an ever deeper conversion is above all praise of the mercy and the saving justice of God.

For the normal Christian the sacrament of penance is not a matter of commandment, not a constant conversion from death to life, but a progressive actualization of baptism, the purification of the heart turned to God, the "second conversion," that is to say an abiding in the light through the constant struggle against darkness.

The sacrament of penance expresses the prayer "Grant us an increase of faith, hope and charity" precisely when it is not obligatory, because the Christian is not conscious of having committed a grave sin. Growth is not a biological process, it is a struggle against evil, a purified praise of God through a humbler life.

Through the grace of God the continual conversion is experienced time and again as a new beginning. This does not mean that a man lives in fear of having lost God's grace. It is the expression of his gratitude because God always says to us again: "Behold, I make all things new." It is a new beginning, because God has given a new grace which renews the heart still more. Progress, however, is not made by smugly looking at the ever more perfect ego, but at Jesus and our neighbor in humble praise and gratitude.

This does not mean that we must not also look at ourselves. For it is the experience of the love of Christ who is really concerned with us, that really helps us to find our true self by turning us back to him and our neighbor.

This continual conversion produces a change of emphasis. Freedom is increasingly experienced as a share in God's freedom, it is ever more synthesized with docility and obedience. At the same time obedience is increasingly seen in relation to the gift of grace, the law seeming ever more clearly an expression of our "life in Christ Jesus."

If we realize that we need a constant conversion we shall also properly understand the law. The new law is the Holy Spirit who awakens and increases in us the love that is the fullness of the law. But we have not yet completely submitted to this law, we have not yet surrendered ourselves wholly to the guidance of the Holy Spirit. Hence we also need the external prescriptions of the law. But these must not be made absolute. They should recall our sinfulness and at the same time lead us to Christ, from whom we expect sanctification and purification. The fruit of our progressive conversion is an increasing synthesis, so that we understand the law truly theologically as a call to humility and to an acceptance of the gifts of the Holy Spirit. Continual conversion is expressed in an increasing spirit of personal responsibility and co-responsibility. It also shows itself in this, that our prayer becomes ever more personal, that it expresses more and more our watching for the coming of the Lord.

The biblical and liturgical renewal has caused the eschatological virtues to move increasingly into the center of ascetical theology.[1] The Christian life is a life of hope, which is nourished by the constant coming of the Lord in grace and by the expectation of his final coming in the Parousia. This is not only to be understood sacramentally. True, the Lord comes to his community and to everyone who receives him in the Eucharist. He is present in every sacrament. But the sacraments do not take the place of Christian life; on the contrary, they give meaning and direction to this life. The Lord comes wherever we meet our neighbor, he comes in all the signs of his providence. The biblical ethic is an ethic of the *kairós,* of the God-given hour. Not we make our plans, but God plans. Christian wisdom is concerned with God's saving plan as it is revealed in revelation itself and in the signs of the times and the events around us, be they great or small.

We can be watchful and truly understand God's plan and the signs of the time only if we have the spirit of prayer. Authentic sacramental piety and the life of prayer manifest themselves in vigilance which is related to the law of grace. Now grace is not opposed to life, but is that inner guide which makes us aware of the call of the hour and the needs of our neighbor. Vigilance is first expressed in gratitude, and gratitude leads to humble obedience to the gifts of God's grace and the call of the hour.

If we consider the life of prayer above all as a carrying out of certain duties we destroy the unity of the Christian life. It is very important that our very language should express the unity between prayer and life. Christian personalism regards faith, hope and love primarily as a dialogue, as human responses. Prayer as an expression of faith, hope and love

---

1. Cf. **Constitution on the Church,** Chapters II and VII: "The Eschatological Nature of the Pilgrim Church."

requires listening to the word of God who speaks as the Creator. Now we do not consider creation as something merely of the past. To the eye of faith creation is the constant presence of the Creator who keeps us alive and directs the destiny of the world. The man who prays listens to Christ and to all the words that come from his lips. He listens to the message of the Church as it presents itself in the life of the saints and in the liturgy. He listens to the commands of just laws; he observes history, God's masterpiece, a history of God with men. Prayer is response and praise, it is a humble effort to understand God better and to answer him ever more adequately. Thus prayer embraces the whole reality of life.

For the Catholic Christian the sacraments are the highlights of prayer. There he is absolutely certain that God speaks to us in Christ Jesus through his Church. There we are most intimately united to the response which the Church, the bride of Christ, makes to her bridegroom. Then personal prayer is united with communal prayer. It is a direct looking towards God, it is availability for God, but always with a view to our life, which is to bear increasing witness to him and his service.

If we regard prayer as a listening and a response, we understand all morality as responsibility in its fullest sense, that is as a listening to God through the situation in which we encounter the love and the need of our neighbor. This responsibility includes in its answer to God the stuff of our life, our own self with our gifts and needs, but above all it includes our neighbor and the community. Thus all our life becomes a prayer of sorts. It is watchfulness, docility, openness and a courageous effort to bring everything back to God, its primary source. This is the full meaning of a Christian ethic of responsibility. It takes all values seriously; it clearly distinguishes the sphere of the world from that of the Church. It admits the multiplicity of duties, values and attitudes. But it is a synthesis, regaining the center of life in Christ.

There is a certain tendency in the Catholic Church to misunderstand the value of actual prayer times, arguing that one's whole life is prayer. This view, however is naively optimistic. Anyone asserting that his whole life has become a prayer would imagine that he has already become perfectly pure and a completely Christian personality. The actual hour of prayer is the direct expression of adoring faith, hope and love. Its value lies in this. At the same time it is absolutely necessary, because it is a factor of integration. A man will be able to make his whole life a response to God only if he makes time for the direct dialogue of prayer. This dialogue is the condition for an authentic encounter with the Thou, just as the daily reverent encounter with our neighbor and our community assures that our encounter with God has a certain fullness and nearness to our life.

The danger of asceticism is to concentrate a man too much on himself and at the same time to provide him with an escape from the true demands of life. Hence we must be particularly careful always to preserve the contact between asceticism and true life in Christ and its demands.

The fundamental norm of Christian asceticism is the paschal mystery of the passion, death and resurrection of the Lord. We must mortify the desires of egocentric man in the power of the Holy Spirit sent to us by the risen Christ. By entrusting himself to the Father, Christ gives himself for the salvation of his brothers. Thus true asceticism is always directed simultaneously to God as an act of loving adoration and to our neighbor as an act of serving love. In this way Christians overcome the wiles of selfish nature and achieve the true freedom of the children of God.

Hence mortification and self-denial do not fight against the
I as such, but only against an egocentric way of life. Mortification does not attack the body, but especially spiritual pride,
self-glorification and self-righteousness. It is, however, also an
effort to subject the body and all the passions to the spirit that
is turned towards Christ.

Asceticism is a life-and-death struggle. If we do not mortify
the desires of Adamitic, egocentric man, we kill the life of
Christ in us. We can overcome the concupiscence of the old
man only in the power of Christ, looking towards him and
trusting in him.

Christian mortification draws its life and vigor from the
joy of Easter. But this can become fully active only if we pay
the price of a constant struggle against selfishness.

The new law is wholly a law of grace and joy. In St. John's
Gospel the Lord introduces the solemn promulgation of the
new law: "Love one another as I have loved you" with the
words: "These things have I spoken to you, that my joy may
be in you, and that your joy may be full" (Jn 15:11). Christian asceticism and Christian existence are in the fullest sense
true to life if they derive from the full truth of the gospel.
Now the center of the gospel is the good news of the resurrection of the Lord who was crucified for us. All asceticism
must express this truth.

The paschal mystery is the fullest expression of victorious
love. Hence asceticism is not something else beside Christian
love, even less does it diminish its energy. Asceticism is true
to life if it affirms the necessity, intrinsic to love, of constant
purification and if it is prepared to make sacrifices which
correspond to the true love of God and neighbor.

Asceticism expresses this love which is still on the purgative
way, hence it will take various forms in the different civiliza-

tions and periods of history according to what best serves the growth of brotherly love. It must always attack those dangers that could harm man's inner freedom and his readiness to serve his neighbor and community.

The *Constitution on the Church in the Modern World* of Vatican II is certainly an impulse to develop the theology of earthly things. But if we seek first the kingdom of God we shall also approach all created things as expressions of God's fatherly love and as means to express our own love for our brothers.

The theology of earthly things and the theology of the world are intimately connected with the meaning of Christian asceticism. Asceticism receives its full truth only from an understanding of the full importance of the world. The world is above all the good creation of God which invites us to praise God and to live in community with our brothers. Against its will, however, the world is tainted by the sin of Adam and his descendants. It is subject to man, who is a sinner. But, being created good by God and, more, redeemed by Christ it calls for redeemed man, who gives it a share in the liberty of the children of God. In St. John the world sometimes also signifies those men who have received the revelation in Jesus Christ and yet decided against him. Asceticism in the Christian sense is a harmonious response to this multiform reality. It is readiness to suffer while resisting the world that is hostile to God. It is readiness to bear witness to Christ in a way that makes it credible to all seekers. It is especially the struggle against our own sinfulness and the contagion of our surroundings, in order once more fully to discover the true meaning of creation.

An asceticism which is true to life responds to the call of reality which wants its full share in the liberty of the children of God. Asceticism is true to life if it is not routine or mere legalism, but open to man's surroundings, open to God's world.

To be this, asceticism must be imbued with the spirit of poverty. By this we do not mean the lack of external possessions, but the attitude that is expressed in the first beatitude: "Blessed are the poor in spirit, for theirs is the kingdom of heaven" (Mt 5:3). To be truly poor in spirit is a gift of the Holy Spirit; he who has it does not lust for possessions. He will arrive at a purified love of all values and all earthly things but not without a struggle against his egoism. Only thus can he be open to the various data in the world, to cultural work, to truly human economic opportunities, to structural reforms and the claims of his neighbors. He who is poor in spirit no longer uses things as mere means. He recognizes that they are gifts of God and hears God's call through them. He is able to discover their true delights, for they are to him a sign of the love of his heavenly Father. But just for this reason they also urge him to reject or change their use if the brotherly community demands it.

Chapters IV and V of the *Constitution on the Church* especially have made it absolutely clear that a truly Christian asceticism cannot be a monopoly of religious. The layman is fully a Christian. Hence all the reasons for asceticism apply equally to laymen, priests and religious. Both the layman living in the world and the Christian living in a religious community must bear witness to the Christian faith and life, even though the emphasis will be different. Perhaps the religious will more obviously testify to the truth that the form of this world is passing away (1 Cor 7:31), while the layman will seek more explicitly to take his share in the work of salvation through serving the secular order; nevertheless, the basic law which both must follow is the perfect truth of God and the world. Their witness must be mutually integrated in such a way that they help each other.

One's attitude to marriage may serve as an example. The celibate state bears witness to the eschatological form of the Christian life in which the setting up of a home and a family cannot be the ultimate goal. The celibate state requires a burning love for Christ and in Christ for every human brother. But the meaning of the celibate life rests on the truth of the great value of marriage and the family. The celibate must know that the fountains of virginal love would dry up if married love did not exist as a redeemed and authentic love. He must know that the Lord does not want him to give up marriage because he despises it. For married people marriage and the family are an authentic way to salvation and sanctity. But, precisely for the sake of marriage, they will also gratefully accept the witness of the celibate. In some way they owe their understanding of the inner freedom in marriage and the family to those who have renounced marriage for the sake of the kingdom of heaven, so that married and parental love accepts the law of purification and growth. The Christian life combines being open to the world and renouncing it, affirming the redeemed world and being prepared to give it up for the salvation of all men. Both aspects are evident in the full affirmation of earthly values and demands in the life of the laity, and the following of the evangelical counsels of voluntary poverty, obedience to a charismatic leader and celibacy for the sake of the kingdom of heaven in the religious life.

6

CHRIST THE FOUNTAIN OF THE NEW LAW OF LOVE

In this last essay the central concern of this whole book is summarized in a form designed to help preachers.

St. Paul and indeed the young Christian communities had often to do with Jewish Christians devoted to the Law, who regarded Christ above all as the "new Moses" who had continued and completed the Mosaic Law. True, they held that Jesus was superior to Moses, but in their opinion his chief importance had been to explain and fulfill the law. But the whole sublimity, beauty and power of the Law of Christ cannot be understood in this way.

New Testament morality is wholly the good news of God's divine love dwelling among us, which transforms our innermost heart, thought and will and thus makes us witnesses of this same love.

This is already clear in the earliest and shortest summary of Christ's preaching transmitted by Mark: "Jesus came into Galilee, preaching the gospel of God, and saying: The time is fulfilled, and the kingdom of God is at hand: repent and believe in the gospel" (Mk 1:14f). God's saving kingdom is close to us in Jesus, who invites us to follow him. Believing in him we recognize the true, infinite love to which we surrender, thus being renewed in our innermost being. Our minds and hearts are renewed in proportion to the gladness and gratitude with which we accept the good news and surrender to him who is the messenger and source of all joy.

In his great synthesis of the moral message of Jesus, St. Matthew alludes to Moses in a way that should not be overlooked. Moses had been separated from his people, and God gave him the tables of the Law to the accompaniment of thunder and lightning. Of Jesus, on the other hand, it is written that he went up to the mountain in view of the crowds and that his disciples came to him. There follows the nine-fold "blessed." God is the source of all joy, all truth, all love. The way of salvation, too, is revealed in the nine beatitudes: in humility, in purifying mourning, in meekness, in hunger and thirst for the righteousness that comes from God, in purity of heart, in the service of peace, if necessary even in the midst of revilings and persecutions for the Lord's sake.

In Christ the disciples too, become the "light of the world" (Mt 5:14). Then follows a series of contrasts: "You have heard that it was said to the men of old.... But I say to you." Now everything is illumined by the love of the heavenly Father who "makes his sun rise on the evil and on the good" (Mt 5:45).

This results in the great, all-embracing law: "You, therefore, must be perfect, as your heavenly Father is perfect" (Mt 5:48). In view of the shortened text in Luke, "Be merciful, even as your Father is merciful" (Lk 6:36), this call to perfection in Matthew may also be interpreted as: "Imitate the goodness of the heavenly Father." In Christ this goodness has become perfectly visible to us. He teaches this infinite love authoritatively by example and word, but most of all by his death.

What is most important, however, is that after the visible victory of his love he sends us the Holy Spirit, thus becoming the source of love for us. "God's love has been poured into our hearts through the Holy Spirit which has been given to us"

(Rom 5:5). Thus the love of Christ urges us from within. We are not under the command of love externally: we know we are loved and we look to this love as our rule of life. We have been taken up into the current of divine love, because Christ lives in us. This is the summary of St. Paul's "gospel": "Christ in us."

All New Testament writings show us Jesus as the fountain of love each in its special way, and through this multiplicity we arrive at a perfect picture. St. John, the beloved disciple, has perhaps been most successful in showing us New Testament morality in the light of this blessed truth. As Matthew in the Sermon of the Mount, so John gives us a comprehensive view of the new law of love in the farewell speeches and the high-priestly prayer.

The Last Supper and thus the comprehensive presentation of Christ's moral message is introduced by the words: "Having loved his own who were in the world, he loved them to the end." Then we are shown the "Lord and Master," visibly teaching humble, serving love through the washing of the feet, and both example and word lead us into the depth of the mystery: "He who has seen me has seen the Father" (Jn 14:9).

Jesus is the final and perfect revelation of the love of the Father. Therefore the new commandment reads in Matthew and Luke: "Be perfect, be good and merciful like your heavenly Father," and in John: "This is my commandment, that you love one another as I have loved you" (Jn 15:12; 13:34). This love is admirably kind and sweet, as we see in the conversation of Jesus with Philip. In his attitude to Judas, who was to betray him, Jesus shows that his love is patient, but not weak; it is serious and decided. This love is frank, it warns in time and steadies the wavering. Look at the way Jesus treats

Peter: first he reproaches him because he refuses to let Jesus wash his feet; then the Lord points out the weakness of the apostle who is so sure of himself and predicts his denial.

Thus we understand the almost breathless account of St. John in his letter: "That which was from the beginning, which we have heard, which we have seen with our eyes, which we have looked upon and touched with our hands, concerning the word of life — the life was made manifest, and we saw it, and testify to it, and proclaim to you the eternal life" (1 Jn 1:1f). From seeing, looking and hearing John goes on to the deeper experience of faith: "That you may have fellowship with us; and our fellowship is with the Father and with his Son, Jesus Christ." And he adds: "We are writing this that our joy be complete" (1 Jn 1:3f).

Immediately before the solemn announcement of the new commandment at the Last Supper "This is my commandment, that you love one another as I have loved you" (Jn 15:12) we read a similar word of Jesus: "These things I have spoken to you, that my joy may be in you, and that your joy may be full" (Jn 15:11). What is this word that gives such joy? It is the message that we have communion with Christ, that he lives in us and we in him, that we thus have fellowship with the Father, together with him. "As the Father has loved me, so have I loved you; abide in my love" (Jn 15:9). Perhaps these words show more clearly than any others that the good news and the commandment are one and that both introduce us deeply into the mystery of our life with Christ. "Abide in my love" gives us the blessed news that we are united to Christ as the branches with the vine. It is both a blissful and an urgent commandment: "Abide in me, and I in you. As the branch cannot bear fruit by itself, unless it abides in the vine, neither can you, unless you abide in me" (Jn 5:4).

The commandment of love is rooted in the good news of Christ, the source of love. Just this gives the commandment its deepest foundation, its firmness and, last but not least, its blissful character. Loving one another with a genuine love, we share in the love that unites Jesus to the Father in heaven (Jn 15:9f). As the Father's commandment to Christ is fulfilled in his infinite love for men, so all individual commandments are included in the love of our neighbor.

We realize the deepest meaning of all virtues and commandments only in an authentic love that has been redeemed and sanctified by Christ.

But what is then the goodness, mercy and kindness of those who do not know Christ? Whence comes their love if they do not even know Christ, the source of love?

It can hardly be doubted that genuine love exists also where Christ is not yet known and worshipped. But if it is genuine it can come only from God, and is certainly also related to Christ. Love which is really directed to a man's neighbor and in harmony with the hierarchy of values shows by its fruits that it is not unredeemed.

The description of the last judgment in Mt 25 gives us a clear indication in this respect. If a man feeds the hungry and visits the sick or prisoners he will be among the elect, even if he was not actually aware of having encountered Christ in his human brothers. It is equally true that all genuine love has not only its origin quite generally in God, but also in Christ, the Savior, so that all true love unites with Christ, its origin.

True, there is something lacking even in a truly strong and pure human love if it does not know its source and ultimate goal explicitly. All those who know Christ as the source of love should be urged by gratitude to make him known among men. But if we really love after the manner of Christ we proclaim him even if we do not actually speak of him. On the other hand, it is a wicked trick to speak of him and yet to deny his love or to hide it completely, for this bars the way to him, who is the source of love. But love leads to its own origin, and then the word that confesses him will be recognized as love.

The genuine disciples of Christ are known by their mutual love. The more their love grows and is purified, the better will they themselves know Christ and help others to look for the source of such love.

Christ proclaims this truth in connection with his great commandment and strongly emphasizes it in the high-priestly prayer. First he prays for those who are specially commissioned to make him known to men: "I have given them the words which thou gavest me, and they have received them and know in truth that I come from thee; and they have believed that thou didst send me ... Holy Father, keep them in thy name, which thou hast given me, that they may be one, even as we are one" (Jn 17:8-11). The "being one"— today we call it collegiality — of the messengers of faith is the fundamental condition for their credibility. But not only bishops and priests are called to proclaim Christ in this way of love and unity. This is asked of all Christians, even though in different ways. Hence the Lord prays: "I do not pray for these only, but also for those who believe in me through their word, that they may all be one ... so that the world may believe that thou hast sent me" (Jn 17:20f).

New Testament morality is inseparable from the gospel and from the messengers, the witnesses of the heavenly Father and is thus the source of love for us. It is also intimately united to the fundamental command to the disciples of Christ to communicate to the world in mutual love the life that goes forth from Christ. The more everything bears witness to this love, the more easily will men discover the truth of the morality of the gospel and thus Christ himself.